RESTORATION GOD'S WAY

Resource Book for Church Leaders

DONALD J. MacNAIR

GREAT COMMISSION PUBLICATIONS

7401 OLD YORK ROAD, PHILADELPHIA, PENNSYLVANIA 19126

ISBN 0-934688-29-X

Printed in U.S.A.

Published by
Great Commission Publications
7401 Old York Road, Philadelphia, Pennsylvania 19126

TABLE OF CONTENTS

PREFACE

Church discipline is part of the ongoing work of God among his people. It is one of the ways that he shows his loving concern for his own. Because he first loved us with an everlasting love, he will graciously lead an offender to repentance, confession and full restoration.

Through this exercise of love, God produces righteousness. This confirms that he is our Father, since he is treating us like sons. Some would say that church discipline is "tough" love, but it is more than that—it is divine love at work.

The Westminster Confession of Faith states that when offenses have been committed, censures are necessary. In chapter 30, section 3, it gives several reasons for using censures. They are:

- to reclaim and gain the offending brethren,
- to deter others from similar offenses,
- to purge out the leaven that might infect the whole lump,
- to vindicate the honor of Christ and the holy profession of the gospel, and
- to prevent the wrath of God from falling upon the church.

This book is based on Paul's instructions in Galatians 6:1, 2: "Brothers, if someone is caught in a sin, you who are spiritual should restore him gently. But watch yourself, or you also may be tempted. Carry each other's burdens, and in this way you will fulfill the law of Christ." We see in this passage that the goal of church discipline is the restoration of the sinner. It must be done firmly, yet "gently," if it is to be successful. And those called upon to administer church discipline must watch themselves, lest they also be tempted.

Believers are often aware of the sins of others and will speak up in love. No formal discipline is needed in such cases, because those who are "spiritual" are able to restore those who have sinned. The context shows that spiritual people are those who "live by the Spirit" (Gal. 5:16). The Holy Spirit indwells them and they strive to follow his leading. The result is that "the fruit of the Spirit" (5:22, 23) is evident in their lives. Christians do not have to have a certain degree of knowledge or a certain amount of involvement in the work of the kingdom in order to be the spiritual brother who speaks to an offender.

Finally, we see in Galatians 6 that effective church discipline must be part of an ongoing ministry of caring. The offender must be fully aware that God is working to enable him to be restored *by* and *within* the family of God. Fellow Christians must carry his burden with him. In this way "the law of Christ" will be fulfilled in the disciplinary process.

This is *restoration God's way*.

By God's grace, formal discipline is not often needed in a healthy church. Members show their concern for other members of the church through loving support and even admonition. Within such a network of concern sin can be prevented or dealt with before it becomes aggravated. This is an expression of love from the body of Christ, and it often leads to repentance.

When this informal process fails, the formal steps of church discipline become necessary. Such action is called judicial discipline.

This book describes both informal and formal church discipline. It examines the biblical principles upon which discipline is based and according to which it is carried out. We provide actual case histories to illustrate these principles. And we show that the Holy Spirit uses church discipline to bring glory to the Lord.

We shall see that when elders administer formal discipline, the Spirit is using them to maintain the purity of the church. He also uses their lives to enhance the exercise of discipline. Their lives of love become an expression of Christ's love in reclaiming his erring children. The disciplinary process also identifies church members whose claim to be saved is contradicted by their unrepentant life.

Three additional subjects are dealt with in this book because of their relevance in today's church. They are:

- the advisability of having "my day in court,"
- the introduction of church discipline in an established church, and
- the avoidance of civil suits.

"Questions for Reflection and Discussion" are provided at the end of each chapter. The book could serve as a study guide for an adult Sunday school class.

Every church that is truly Christian will try to do what Christ and his disciples instruct it to do in the Bible. How well it does so will indicate how healthy it is. This implies that its members will want to practice holiness as their way of life and, when necessary, will defend the name of Christ against offense and sin.

The church knows that it is a body of sinners saved by grace. So while it has been freed from the bondage of sin, it must constantly overcome the remaining presence and power of sin. The church also knows that the Lord has revealed in the Bible how to overcome offenses and remove sin.

The purpose of this book is to encourage churches to practice, and their members to accept, biblical church discipline as an integral part of healthy church life.

Donald J. MacNair
December 1986

1

INTRODUCING CHURCH DISCIPLINE

Church discipline is divine love at work! It is the work of God producing "a harvest of righteousness and peace for those who have been trained by it" (Heb. 12:11). It is God's demonstration that he loves us as children of his grace, adopted into his family.

The Bible over and over again asserts that the Christian must persevere in holiness and in fighting against sin in his life. The writer of Hebrews tells us how much is required: "In your struggle against sin, you have not yet resisted to the point of shedding your blood" (12:4). The Christian may have to struggle as hard as a boxer who has been bloodied but will not give up. Such perseverance is ultimately a source of blessing from God. It is his way of training us as his sons.

When God disciplines us, he is still our Father. His purpose for our lives does not change, either. Discipline is an expression of his fatherly love, by which he produces the fruit of righteousness and peace. This is brought out in these passages:

"Remember how the Lord your God led you all the way in the desert ... to humble you and to test you .... He humbled you, causing you to hunger and then feeding you with manna ... to teach you that man does not live on bread alone but on every word that comes from the mouth of the Lord.... Know then in your heart that as a man disciplines his son, so the Lord your God disciplines you" (Deut. 8:2, 3, 5).

"My son, do not despise the Lord's discipline and do not resent his rebuke, because the Lord disciplines those he loves, as a father the son he delights in" (Prov. 3:11, 12).

"Endure hardship as discipline; God is treating you as sons. For what son is not disciplined by his father?" (Heb. 12:7).

Church elders have no choice but to exercise discipline when it is necessary. When they do so properly, as shepherds and guardians, they demonstrate the love that God has for his church. Indeed, God holds them accountable for this (Heb. 13:17).

Elders also have a responsibility to prepare the church for discipline. There must be ongoing education and training in church discipline. Elders can contribute the most to this preparation by working to develop unity, life and a support network of concern within the body.

Certain premises are basic to the proper administration of church discipline. One is that every offense is in fact an offense against Christ and his church. Therefore, the only two parties in a disciplinary case are the church and the defendant.

Another premise is that church discipline may be instituted only when someone is charged with doing something that is prohibited by Scripture.

There are three reactions to church discipline that must be prevented or overcome by careful planning and shepherding. Otherwise, the church will not be able to exercise loving concern for its members when they need discipline.

The first undesirable reaction is that church members leave the church before submitting to discipline. This often happens when people have been improperly motivated to be "part of the body." Too often they are motivated only to fulfill their felt needs and to enjoy fellowship. These are important aspects of church life, but the primary motivation for being part of the church must be to worship God regularly with other believers. Unless personal fulfillment and fellowship are grounded in corporate worship, the motive for church membership will be undermined by the prospect of discipline. Thus, members with improper motivation will usually "run away" from it.

The second undesirable reaction is that church members do not really forgive and restore an offender who has repented. Sometimes members express their forgiveness, but it does not show up consistently in the life of the church. Too often there is an element of hidden distrust.

The third undesirable reaction is a failure to achieve reconciliation when an accused person has been found not guilty. In this situation the accuser must seek reconciliation, and possibly even recant his accusation, before the case can be truly settled. Until then, the body of believers is still in anguish. Proper discipline requires that a dispute be fully resolved before the Lord.

Two principles must be taught in order to foster proper attitudes toward church discipline. In the first place, each Christian must remember that Jesus Christ died for him so that God would forgive his sins. Ephesians 4:32 says it all: "Be kind and compassionate to one another, forgiving each other, just as in Christ God forgave you." If God has forgiven you, you certainly can—and must—forgive your brother.

The other principle that must be kept in mind is that every offense is an offense against God. No matter how much people may be hurt, every offense is basically a rebellion against God himself. Only when the Christian sees his brother's offense in that light will he be able to freely forgive. These two

11

principles cannot be separated. They work together.

The church must help its members to realize that they are meeting with the living God when they worship. This realization fosters a deeper relationship with God, in which his blessings are increasingly appreciated. The joy of such a relationship makes unity with God's other children and obedience to God's word a natural part of living.

The elders who administer church discipline and the members who subject themselves to it must keep in mind that church courts do not operate like our civil courts. The church elders, who become the "court," appoint one of their own to be the prosecutor, and they serve as the judge, the jury and the administrators of judicial censure. This reflects the fact that the church is not a democracy, but a monarchy—a kingdom—ruled by Jesus Christ, and that the elders are his representatives. This must be taught to church members as they mature in the life of the church.

Church discipline presupposes that church members

- meet with the living God in regular worship,

- subject themselves to their elders to be blessed by God,

- have been taught at least the basic principles of church discipline and the way it works, and

- experience love as the essence of church discipline, in practice as well as in promise.

Unless these premises are operative in the life of the church, the exercise of church discipline may create as many problems as it solves. Conversely, if these premises become a natural part of church life, the Holy Spirit will use church discipline to bring about the repentance and restoration of offenders, to strengthen the life and unity of the body, and to maintain or enhance the purity of the church.

Questions for Reflection and Discussion

1. Why is it proper to say that church discipline is an expression of God's fatherly love?

2. In what ways would you like to see your fellow church members instructed and trained in the concepts of church discipline?

3. How do church courts operate differently than our civil courts? How do you feel about this?

2

SUPPORT-NETWORK CONCERN

Church discipline is "the exercise of authority given the Church by the Lord Jesus Christ to instruct and guide its members and to promote its purity and welfare" (*The Book of Church Order of the Presbyterian Church in America*, § 27–1).

This is a good, standard definition of church discipline. Christ's love for his church is expressed through church discipline whenever its purity and welfare are threatened. In this way he reaches out to reclaim his erring children and protects his people from the trouble that comes when unrepentant sinners are included in their fellowship. The Holy Spirit uses the church itself to do this.

In most situations the Spirit starts the disciplinary process by using the love of Christian brothers for each other. Such love is a natural characteristic of a healthy church (i.e., a church that is reasonably conformed to the New Testament model). Notice how this love expresses itself.

As a church grows in unity and spiritual maturity, its members become more and more like Christ, and therefore increasingly concerned for each other. They are being built up in love. The church lives with the anticipation that God will bless it with spiritual growth. Spiritual growth is evidenced by the increasingly holy lives of its individual members and the deepening unity of the body as a whole, especially where purity of life and doctrine is concerned.

Paul makes this the norm for a church. In Ephesians 4:16 he states: "From him the whole body, joined and held together by every supporting ligament, grows and builds itself up in love, as each part does its work."

Both unity and purity are threatened and quickly hurt when a member fails to resist temptation. In Ephesians 4:14 Paul warns that sin will produce *heresy* ("every wind of teaching") and *immorality* ("the cunning and craftiness of men in their deceitful scheming"—cf. Titus 1:10–16, especially vs. 15). The Christian, especially the immature one, is vulnerable to the attack of sin. He is like an infant adrift at sea, "tossed back and forth by the waves." He needs help. So Paul directs the church to reach out and restore him: "Brothers, if someone is caught in a sin, you who are spiritual should restore him gently. But watch yourself, or you also may be tempted" (Gal. 6:1).

Explicit in the apostle's charge is a member-to-member ministry of concern. When they see Satan attack, fellow Christians are to *speak out:* they are to speak the *truth* and do so in *love* (Eph. 4:15). This means that they encourage and comfort one another. They share the word of God along with their own experiences of trial and God-granted victory. They also rebuke and admonish. Again, they share the word and, when possible, tell how they were tempted and how they responded to the admonition given to them. Such concern is the foundation upon which church discipline is built. This is a healthy church functioning at its best.

As the pastor/teacher equips the church for ministry and the members respond by ministering, the usual result is that the whole body grows in Christ. The bond of fellowship is also strengthened, which in turn leads to an even more effective support network. As a result, probably 80 percent of all the disciplinary problems that arise in a healthy church are resolved in a quiet and often private expression of bold love between members.

Such support must be given carefully. It cannot be an expression of ignorance or superficial judgment. It cannot be motivated by a need to gratify one's ego. It must separate truth from personal opinions. It must be the voice of a friend, serving in love.

There is danger involved in support-network concern, but the risk is far outweighed by the benefits. The risk is minimized when the pastor/teacher properly equips the church members and makes them aware of their responsibility to practice loving support using the wisdom provided by the Holy Spirit.

Such support is given with the assurance that God will provide the member being tempted with the strength to withstand the temptation and will provide the member who has sinned with the strength to repent of his sin. The supporter knows that his admonition and encouragement are based on the victory that each Christian has over the power of sin. Paul tells us that the power of sin has been broken by the death and resurrection of Christ, even though the presence of sin has not been removed: "If we have been united with him ... in his death, we will certainly also be united with him in his resurrection. For we know that our old self was crucified with him so that the body of sin might be done away with, that we should no longer be slaves to sin" (Rom. 6:5, 6). He goes on to say: "Therefore do not let sin reign in your mortal body so that you obey its evil desires. Do not offer the parts of your body to sin, as instruments of wickedness, but rather offer yourselves to God, as those who have been brought from death to life" (vss. 12, 13).

In Matthew's gospel, Jesus provides practical applications of this truth. He mentions two common situations where personal offense is involved (which is where support-network

17

concern most often works), and tells Christians what to do about them.

In the first case, the action of one person has disturbed someone else's conscience, offending him and God. (The offended party should be primarily concerned that God, not he himself, has been offended. Otherwise, it becomes almost impossible to forgive when the opportunity arises.) Jesus makes crystal clear what must be done. When the offender finds out about it, he is to go to the offended party, confess his sorrow at being offensive, and seek reconciliation: "Therefore, if you are offering your gift at the altar and there remember that your brother has something against you, leave your gift there in front of the altar. First go and be reconciled to your brother; then come and offer your gift" (Matt. 5:23, 24).

If the commands of Jesus are disregarded, the church may have to proceed with judicial discipline. Support-network concern often motivates the offender to obey the Scriptures and thus avoid judicial discipline. If such concern is not expressed, the situation often worsens to the point where church discipline (which is always perceived as more severe than the expression of concern from a network of believers) must be administered.

In Jesus' second example, a Christian believes he has been sinned against. Again, Jesus speaks clearly: "If your brother sins against you, go and show him his fault, just between the two of you. If he listens to you, you have won your brother over. But if he will not listen, take one or two others along, so that 'every matter may be established by the testimony of two or three witnesses.' If he refuses to listen to them, tell it to the church ..." (Matt. 18:15–17).

This procedure was followed in the following case, and repentance was accomplished before the latter part of the passage had to be invoked. Once when a church was being built, a small electronic organ was donated. Everyone was thrilled, especially the organist. Shortly before the service of dedication, the donor made it known that her granddaughter, rather than the organist, was to play the organ at that service. This created such tension that the unity of the church was threatened. The donor's behavior was perceived as a sinful act of pride, especially because of previous difficulties between the donor and the organist. The elders prepared to visit the donor, give the organ back, and begin disciplinary action. They also planned to go to the organist and instruct her in using the Matthew 18 directive. But before they could do so, another member of the church urged the organist to go to the donor at once and confront her. She did so, and the donor repented. The donor apologized for taking such a shortsighted, self-gratifying and proud attitude. As a result, the tension in the church was replaced with rejoicing. Network support had motivated a person-to-person ministry and the Holy Spirit brought about repentance and restoration without any need for formal discipline.

It should be noted that if the problem had not been resolved, the organist would have been obligated to visit the donor again, this time taking along one or two witnesses. At this point the support network often must step in again and urge the offended party to carry out the scriptural mandate to its completion.

Church discipline is to proceed within the context of prayer (Matt. 18:19). Similarly, network support must be bathed in prayer. It is wrong to speak out, even in love, without doing so prayerfully. The word spoken in love must be perceived to come from a concerned, gentle heart. The message must be presented as from the Lord.

The importance of prayer is brought out in Philippians 4, where Paul speaks the truth to Euodia and Syntyche (vs. 2) and then calls on the church to rejoice always and pray about everything with thanksgiving (vs. 4). "Everything" includes the confrontation with the two women. The church would thus be free of anxiety (vs. 4). It is important to note that Paul's grounds for doing all this are that he has already prayed for them (Phil. 1:3, 7).

Prayer not only precedes speaking, but also characterizes the entire experience. No one who speaks the truth in love dare lose the sense of urgency that motivated him to speak out in the first place. He does not have the option to let up in his prayer support just because the process has begun or because he is no longer the central figure in developing it. The entire process of member-to-member concern and its consequences must be bathed in prayer.

More churches need to build up support networks. When new members are brought into the body, stress must be placed on the benefits that come from supporting one another on a personal level. Elders are responsible to take a lead in this, since they are called upon to keep watch over the flock (Acts 20:28).

In 1 Corinthians 12, Paul states that no one (elders included) is superior to anyone else, and that no one (such as the newest Christian) is inferior. In this context Paul shows that the gifts and talents of every member have value for the whole body: "But in fact God has arranged the parts in the body, every one of them, just as he wanted them to be" (vs.18). New Christians certainly need the elders and the other mature members, but the mature members also benefit from the babes in Christ. Any member of the body may need the concern which the support network provides. Everyone should know that he is part of such a network.

Questions for Reflection and Discussion

1. What are two general categories of sin? List at least four examples of each.

2. What is church discipline? Discuss how discipline promotes purity and the welfare of the congregation.

3. What are the ways in which support-network concern is usually expressed? Share with others how you have been tempted and how God has enabled you to overcome the temptation.

4. How can the misuse of support-network concern hurt a Christian undergoing temptation?

5. What two cases of personal offense does Jesus specifically deal with? Explain when Matthew 18:15–17 should be used. What are some possible dangers of ignoring these directives or of not following them specifically as given?

6. How could you start or strengthen the support-network ministry of your church?

3

APPRECIATING CHURCH PURITY
FROM GOD'S POINT OF VIEW

"Expel the wicked man from among you" (1 Cor. 5:13). Frightening words! But in the church at Corinth a man had his father's wife (vs. 1). And worse yet, church members were proud of their tolerance of the sin (vs. 2). They even boasted about it (vs. 6)!

But Paul, for the good of the man and of the church, commanded that he be disciplined: "When you are assembled in the name of our Lord Jesus and I am with you in spirit, and the power of our Lord Jesus is present, hand this man over to Satan, so that the sinful nature may be destroyed and his spirit saved on the day of the Lord" (1 Cor. 5:4, 5). The church was further commanded to change its ways: "But now I am writing you that you must not associate with anyone who calls himself a brother but is sexually immoral or greedy, an idolater or a slanderer, a drunkard or a swindler" (vs. 11). Paul longed to see the offender brought to repentance and restoration and the church committed to holiness.

When support-network concern is either not put to use or not effective, or when a gross crime or heresy is involved, God uses judicial discipline to vindicate his name. It calls the offender to repentance and brings purity to the body. Since Scripture reveals that the church is commanded and empowered to use it, it must not be ignored or excused away.

In Matthew 16:19 Jesus promises to provide keys to the kingdom of God in order to build his church. Certain keys—preaching, admission into the body, the sacraments and worship—provide access to the kingdom. Another one—discipline—bars access to it. (See *The Challenge of the Eldership*, by Donald J. MacNair [Philadelphia: Great Commission Publications, 1984], pp. 32, 33.) Peter (Matt. 16:19) and then all the disciples (John 20:23) were given the keys. In Matthew 18:18 Jesus instructs the church (through its elders) to use them. In 1 Corinthians 5:4 Paul commands a congregation to use them in a specific case. Hebrews 13:17 indicates that elders will be held accountable to the Lord for their use of the keys.

Christ instituted the keys of the kingdom for a high purpose: to "build my church" (Matt. 16:18). He has begun a good work in each Christian and will "carry it on to completion until the day of Christ Jesus" (Phil. 1:6), when he will present to himself "a radiant church, without stain or wrinkle or any other blemish, but holy and blameless" (Eph. 5:27). He accomplishes this through the Holy Spirit, who works through the Bible, the congregation of believers, the elders and providence. This goal is so important to God that he is using the church *right now* to demonstrate his manifold wisdom "to the rulers and authorities in the heavenly realms" (Eph. 3:10).

Paul instructs Titus to use the key of discipline. Rebellious people, who are teaching false doctrine and seeking personal gain at the expense of others, are to be sharply rebuked (Titus 1:10–13). A divisive person is to have two warnings, after which Titus is to have nothing more to do with him (3:9–11). Titus is to deal with such an offender in the name of the church, so that the families of the church will not be led astray, the offender will be led to repentance, and the name of Christ will be vindicated.

Church members are to be in submission to their elders, who are to guard them against any need for discipline and correct them by the exercise of it (Heb. 13:17). Submission is an attitude of the heart. Based on the conviction that God's blessing is given to those who obey him (1 Pet. 1:1, 2), it is "the posture in which obedience is able to work" (*The Challenge of the Eldership*, p. 36). Submission is the heart willingly saying: "It is in the practice of biblical submission that I will most readily find God's blessing, under the servant-leadership of him whom God holds accountable for my well-being."

The Scriptures reveal another reason to practice submission: we must all appear before the judgment seat of Christ. Now Christians have been adopted into God's family and are enrolled in the Lamb's book of life, and so we should have no fear of the condemnation reserved for the lost. However, our works will be judged to see whether or not they bring glory to God (2 Cor. 5:10; 1 Cor. 3:12–15; Rev. 20:12, 15).

Many people in the church are afraid of judicial discipline. Their fears should be minimized or even removed, however, once they realize what limitations the word of God places on the use of the keys. The main limitation is that they may not be used in temporal ways, since the church is a spiritual kingdom. Jesus declares: "Give to Caesar what is Caesar's, and to God what is God's" (Matt. 22:21), and "My kingdom is not of this world" (John 18:36).

Judicial discipline, then, is limited to the infliction of censures which withhold spiritual blessings. But even when the offender is removed from the church, the purpose is to bring about repentance and restoration, never simply to "get rid of the troublesome offender." As Dr. C. John Miller once put it, the purpose of biblical church discipline is to get the offender to understand the cross from God's point of view.

Judicial discipline is further limited by the requirement that elders proceed with the right attitude of heart. This is of such great importance that it will be discussed at length later.

25

The tender heart of the elder enables the exercise of church discipline to be a means of blessing. He must be responsive to the will of God and sympathetic to the plight of the offender.

Questions for Reflection and Discussion

1. Why must judicial discipline be used when sin has been exposed and is not repented of?

2. What are the keys of the kingdom, and why are they used? Who is to use them? Give three or more examples, either from your own experience or in the New Testament, in which each of the keys was used.

3. According to the Bible, what is the purpose for submission? How does it apply in the elder-member relationship?

4. What limitations are placed on the use of judicial discipline in the church? Why has God put these limitations into place? Discuss how they should relieve the anxiety that may result from a church's commitment to practice judicial discipline when necessary.

4

DISCIPLINE AND CHURCH PEACE, UNITY AND PURITY

Church discipline is designed to build up the members of the church. Paul explained to the Corinthians: "This is why I write these things when I am absent, that when I come I may not have to be harsh in my use of authority—the authority the Lord gave me for building you up, not for tearing you down" (2 Cor. 13:10).

There are three uses of discipline in the church. First, there is administrative discipline, by which the general administration of the church and its ministry are managed. Second, there is corrective discipline, by which misunderstandings about administrative discipline, and breakdowns of it, are corrected. Third, there is judicial discipline, by which repentance and restoration are sought through the imposition of censures. Administrative discipline initiates and controls, while corrective and judicial discipline respond to undesirable developments. A church may appear to be strong in almost all areas of its life, but if all three types of discipline are not being exercised, the church will never be able to experience its potential for peace, unity and purity.

Elders have the task of exercising administrative discipline. Paul says that they are called to "direct the affairs of the church," and that they are "worthy of double honor" if they do it well (1 Tim. 5:17). The elders must make sure that the church is properly carrying out all its biblical functions. They must ensure that each area of ministry has proper leadership, organization, standards, goals, funding, evaluation and feedback. This will not only provide an ordered and fulfilling church experience, but also challenge the members to live for the glory and enjoyment of God.

Administrative discipline also provides elders with the credentials of leadership that they will need when they must exercise responsive (i.e., corrective and judicial) discipline. This can be very important, for if elders have not established their leadership role in the congregation, it will be difficult to proceed effectively with responsive discipline. It will then appear to be an unwanted interference with private prerogatives, rather than a loving expression of mercy.

When misunderstandings or other problems of church administration make corrective discipline necessary, it is usually because differences of opinion have arisen, not because the basic concepts of government or administration are being challenged. Nonetheless, if such tensions are not relieved, they may become so aggravated that judicial discipline becomes necessary. Support-network concern relieves the tension beautifully in many of these situations. Occasionally, however, specific action by the elders is necessary. Promptness is the first requirement for such action. Very often the best way to begin solving the problem is to have all the parties hear each other out before any decisions are made.

Some of the areas that most often require corrective discipline are:

- the volunteer choir

- building, renovation and redecorating programs

- decisions about missionary support (who and how much)

- changes in the order of Sunday morning worship
- leadership techniques
- leadership which was not at first limited by specific parameters
- poor administration
- poor communication
- judgments regarding the qualifications of candidates for office

As a safeguard against misunderstanding, the elders should teach the following truths to the members of the church (including all new members):

- All Christians have the same Savior and the same salvation.
- All Christians have the same Lord.
- All Christians have the same Bible and therefore the same revelation of who God is and what he expects of us.
- *But*, each Christian has his own unique experience and personality, and he sees God's will for himself first and foremost through that grid.
- *Therefore*, Christians must expect differences of opinion to surface, and so should not become hostile simply because they arise. Rather, Christians must continue to communicate until they reach an agreement (presuming, of course, that no moral or doctrinal principle is at stake).

Paul has this in mind in Philippians 4:2: "I plead with Euodia and I plead with Syntyche to agree with each other in the Lord." He warns against foolish arguments, especially in light of the faithfulness of God: "Warn them before God against quarreling about words; it is of no value, and only ruins those who listen" (2 Tim. 2:14).

Misunderstandings that need a response are constantly surfacing. Too often elders view them as either too unimportant or too personal for them to deal with. As a result, such problems are usually ignored, passed off to someone else, or given only cursory attention and then forgotten. Or, elders view them as a recurring source of frustration and guilt, which in turn makes it difficult for them to function efficiently. True, care must be taken not to allow minor things to be considered major. But, care must surely be taken not to allow minor things to *become* major.

A difficult problem once arose in a church of about 300 members. Because of disagreements with the policies of a missions board, the elders of the church decided to support a different mission. At that time the church was completely supporting a missionary who was serving under the board in question. Since the church had complete confidence in the missionary himself, he was asked to change to another missions board. He agreed to do so, and left for the field, but later changed his mind. The elders then proposed to the congregation that they maintain his salary for one year and guarantee him (and the foreign government involved) as much funding as would be necessary for his return to the United States, whenever he wanted to come back.

Realizing how much difference of opinion and resulting tension had been generated by their proposal, the elders called for a meeting at which there was no power to make any motions or vote. They digested the response at that meeting and made a few refinements in their original proposal, but did not make any radical changes in it. They called for a second meeting, again with no power to move or vote. Then a third meeting was called, at which the motion was made and the vote was taken. Many of the differences of opinion still remained, but the tension had been removed by the discussion. The vote sustained the recommendation of the elders. The meeting was concluded with the singing of "Blest Be the Tie That Binds."

Occasionally, because of unrepented offense or sin, judicial discipline is necessary. Its purpose is threefold. First, it seeks to reclaim the offender: "Rebuke them sharply, so that they will be sound in the faith" (Titus 1:13).

Second, it seeks to purify the church: "Those who sin are to be rebuked publicly, so that the others may take warning" (1 Tim. 5:20; see also 1 Cor. 5:6, 7). Paul deals with this in 2 Corinthians 13:2, 3: "I already gave you a warning when I was with you the second time. I now repeat it while absent: On my return I will not spare those who sinned earlier or any of the others, since you are demanding proof that Christ is speaking through me." Paul will spare neither "those who sinned earlier" nor "any of the others." The "others" would be offenders who were not previously identified and those who have been drawn into sin because of the sin of those previously identified.

Third, judicial discipline seeks to vindicate the name of Christ: "For we are to God the aroma of Christ among those who are being saved and those who are perishing" (2 Cor. 2:15).

One evangelical church faced up to the challenge of judicial discipline when a teenage girl who belonged to the church insisted on living with a married man. Her parents had brought her up to love Christ. Her rebellion was devastating to the family and shocked the church. The elders visited her and admonished her. When no repentance was evident, they suspended her. Finally, they excommunicated her.

The decision was a hard one. At least one elder admitted privately that he wondered if the church was only driving an insurmountable wedge between her and the church. In accordance with his ordination vows, however, when the elders voted to proceed he went along with the decision and worked to make it a spiritual act, not just the satisfaction of the letter of the law. The church was hurt. It continued to pray for her, even after she moved out of state.

Three years later, from a city halfway across the country, the elders received a letter from her. She was returning for a visit and very much wanted to worship with the church. The Lord had led her into full repentance as a direct (though delayed) consequence of the church's action. She asked permission to meet with the elders before the service in order to tell them about her repentance and victory in Christ. It was a great day in the church! The church had vindicated the name of Christ from the outset and had accepted its responsibility to maintain the purity of the body, and now it received the blessing of seeing a member's repentance and restoration in God's own time.

Judicial discipline has a related purpose: to prevent the consequences of not vindicating the name of Christ. That is, judicial discipline keeps the church from suffering the wrath of God: "That is why many among you are weak and sick, and a number of you have fallen asleep. But if we judged ourselves, we would not come under judgment" (1 Cor. 11:30, 31).

This is a recurring theme in the Bible. Jeremiah refers to it often. For example, he quotes this admonition from the Lord: "Administer justice every morning; rescue from the hand of his oppressor the one who has been robbed, or my wrath will break out and burn like fire ..." (21:12). The church faces punishment if it ignores or mishandles discipline, just as Israel was punished at Ai because of Achan's sin (Josh. 7). But once Achan was disciplined, God blessed Israel. Similarly, when the church vindicates Christ's name today, it avoids God's wrath, and that is a blessing indeed.

But before discipline can bring blessing (rather than disruption) to the body of believers, there must be faith that God will indeed change men through discipline. Even more, there must be faith that God is able to do what seems impossible to men—all, of course, for his glory. The officers who exercise church discipline and the members who receive it must be able to say this: "Now to him who is able to do immeasurably more than all we ask or imagine, according to his power that is at work within us, to him be glory in the church and in Christ Jesus throughout all generations, for ever and ever! Amen" (Eph. 3:20, 21).

Discipline provides the church with an opportunity to

mature through forgiving the penitent sinner and reaffirming its love for him. The church that fails to forgive may cause the offender to be "overwhelmed by excessive sorrow" (2 Cor. 2:7). Satan, with his evil scheming, will have won a great victory at the expense of the glory of God.

The church that does reach out with love and forgiveness will experience afresh (corporately and individually) the love of Christ for each member. This is one of the best ways to keep the first love of each member very much alive. It usually produces rapid spiritual growth in the church.

By exercising discipline, the church demonstrates to the world that it really does love God. As Jesus says, "By this all men will know that you are my disciples, if you love one another" (John 13:35). John adds: "If anyone obeys his word, God's love is truly made complete in him" (1 John 2:5), and "This is love for God: to obey his commands" (5:3). The Christian experiences the love of God being completed in him, so that he is a better reflection of Christ than before his participation in the process of discipline.

The practice and results of judicial discipline show the world that the living Christ is at work in his church and that the church takes the glory of her Lord seriously.

When all the forms of biblical church discipline are used regularly in the life of the church, it will be ready to develop its full potential for peace, unity and purity. Such a church is a blessing to the name of the Lord.

Questions for Reflection and Discussion

1. How does administrative discipline build up the church? How is it often misused, with the result that the church is torn down instead of built up?

2. What seven things must each area of church ministry have? Discuss them from the point of view of initiating and from the point of view of controlling.

3. What are the two kinds of responsive discipline? Give at least one illustration of each.

4. How does the guideline for avoiding interpersonal hostilities work? Give a specific example.

5. What do Titus 1:13, 1 Timothy 5:20 and 2 Corinthians 13:2, 3 teach about vindicating the name of Christ?

5

OFFENSE CANNOT BE IGNORED

When the Christian does what the Bible tells him not to do, or when he does not do what it tells him to do, he has sinned. He has offended God, the name of Christ, and his church, whether or not anyone knows about it.

An offense is anything in doctrine or practice which is contrary to the word of God. According to the Westminster Confession of Faith, "The whole counsel of God concerning all things necessary for his own glory, man's salvation, faith and life, is either expressly set down in Scripture, or by good and necessary consequence may be deduced from Scripture" (chap. 1, sect. 6). Thus, it is a sin not only to commit murder (Ex. 20:13), but also not to avoid practices "which tend to the unjust taking away the life of any" (Larger Catechism, Q. 135).

It is proper to institute disciplinary measures only when an action can be proved to be contrary to Scripture. On occasion someone is offended by an action that is not contrary to the word of God. Every effort should be made to heal the hurt. However, once a Christian's action has been identified in Scripture as an offense, it must be repented of or disciplined. It cannot be ignored.

When censuring an offender, the church must be careful to administer discipline that takes the nature of the offense into account, since every offense does not warrant the same severity of punishment. Thus, Jesus told the inhabitants of Korazin that God's judgment would be more bearable for Tyre and Sidon than for them: "Woe to you, Korazin! Woe to you, Bethsaida! If the miracles that were performed in you had been performed in Tyre and Sidon, they would have repented long ago in sackcloth and ashes. But I tell you, it will be more bearable for Tyre and Sidon on the day of judgment than for you" (Matt. 11:21, 22).

The parties who are offended make a difference in the severity of the censure. For example, when a person loses his temper and shouts, he offends those around him. But when he adds profanity to that shouting, he also offends God, and thus deserves a more severe punishment. Similarly, when someone ridicules a church member for making some mistakes while trying to serve the Lord, he commits an offense. But when he ridicules a babe in Christ, he is subject to more severe punishment.

The severity of chastisement for the same offense varies according to the knowledge, spiritual maturity and responsibilities of the offender. Jesus makes it clear that we are held accountable to use whatever knowledge we have: "That servant who knows his master's will and does not get ready or does not do what his master wants will be beaten with many blows. But the one who does not know and does things deserving punishment will be beaten with few blows" (Luke 12:47, 48). Likewise, when a Christian who is young in the faith sins, he is not normally punished with the same degree of severity as an elder who does the same thing. Both will be punished, but the elder is presumed to know more about the person and work of Christ and the joy of walking in obedience to him. He is supposed to be an example to the flock (1 Tim. 4:12). James declares: "Not many of you should presume to be teachers, my brothers, because you know that we who teach will be judged more strictly" (3:1).

Finally, the circumstances of the offense may aggravate it in the sight of God and therefore demand a more severe censure. For example, the so-called little white lie is a sin, but the same lie deserves a more severe punishment under some circumstances. For instance, someone may play a practical joke on a friend by saying, "There's a fire in the building!"—meaning that there is a fire in the furnace. If this causes personal distress, it takes on the character of an offense. But if someone with the same motive were to shout the same words in a crowded room and cause a stampede in which people were injured, he would be subject to a much more severe punishment.

Certain categories of offense have been occurring more frequently in the church since the middle of this century. For example, many people no longer regard chastity before and during marriage as a binding standard. Regardless of popular opinion, however, it is a biblical principle and must therefore be maintained (Matt. 19:4–6). Since the church is "the pillar and foundation of the truth" (1 Tim. 3:15) in the world, it must call upon people to obey God. It must treat unbiblical behavior in this area as offense.

A problem of this sort was well handled recently in an evangelical church. An engineering student had a premarital affair with a coed, and she became pregnant. When the pastor learned the details from the father of the young man, he informed the elders that a gross sin had been committed within the membership of the church. They decided to ask the pastor to appoint two of their number to work with him in seeking to lead the offenders to repentance. It was agreed that they would not be given the details at that time, but that if there was no evidence of repentance within two weeks, the elders would be called upon to institute formal disciplinary action. They all committed themselves to prayer.

After several meetings with the offenders, no evidence of repentance was forthcoming. They were then informed that formal action would soon begin. However, the roots of their faith and the love and concern of the church were used by the Holy Spirit to move each of them to a genuine expression of repentance within the time set by the elders. They were soon married, and the young man went to work to support his family while completing his education in night school.

Many such cases work out well, but some do not. For instance, in a church of about 150 members, a married couple separated because they were "incompatible." The elders attempted to bring about a reconciliation, but to no avail. The wife sued for and was granted a divorce. The elders placed her under discipline, which eventually led to her excommunication.

Because of the number of offenses in this one area alone, every elder should familiarize himself with the key biblical texts about marriage and divorce. They are Deuteronomy 24:1–4; Matthew 5:31, 32; 19:3–9; Mark 10:2–12; Luke 16:18; Romans 7:1–3; 1 Corinthians 7:10–16.

In a similar vein, the church must deal with the sin of homosexuality more and more frequently. The position now often taken is that a homosexual person is born with a psychological bent in that direction, and therefore cannot be held responsible for it. Some will agree that it is sinful to practice homosexuality, but few consider homosexual orientation itself to be sinful. But this is not the position of the Bible. Paul states: "Men committed indecent acts with other men, and received in themselves the due penalty for their perversion" (Rom. 1:27). Scripture teaches, then, that the attitude itself is a perversion. It is wrong to hold that the grace of God need not or cannot change the homosexual person.

This problem arose in a church when it discovered that its paid organist was a practicing homosexual. He was fired, whereupon he sued the church for an astronomical sum of money. He claimed that his rights as a citizen had been violated. Evangelical churches across the country helped to pay the legal fees. The church was right, even though the world disagreed. The church won the case.

Another offense that is increasingly common, yet too often is not effectively dealt with by the expression of support-network concern, is drunkenness. Regardless of one's view on the use of alcoholic beverages, drunkenness is a sin. Paul states: "The acts of the sinful nature are obvious: ... drunkenness ..." (Gal. 5:19, 21; cf. 1 Cor. 5:11). This sin must not be ignored, regardless of our culture's permissive attitude toward it.

Still another offense on the increase today is heresy. God, in his wisdom, made the major doctrines of the faith stand out clearly throughout the Bible. Other doctrines, all part of our system of doctrine, are supported by relating Scripture to Scripture. Today the church is facing heresy in all areas of doctrine. Many professing Christians are content to accept as their standard of truth only those things that they happen to "feel good" about. It is heresy to accept anything but the Bible as *the* standard of faith and practice. This is a difficult offense to deal with, but it cannot be condoned.

Elders should be particularly prepared to minister in these troublesome areas, recognizing that God's power to bring about repentance is not diminished in our day.

Many times offenses are dealt with by the support network of fellow members. But sometimes judicial discipline is needed. There are those who sincerely believe that the cost of church discipline is too great, but no cost compares to the reproach brought to the name of Christ when the church does not deal with sin in its midst. Offense cannot be ignored.

Questions for Reflection and Discussion

1. What is the danger when a standard other than the Bible is used to declare an act to be an offense?

2. What four considerations affect the degree of severity with which discipline is to be administered for an offense? Give an illustration of each one.

3. What four categories of offense are occurring more frequently in the church today? How did the elders handle the

case of the engineering student? How is that example relevant to your church?

4. In what ways do many Christians use culture or personal preference as the standard by which they make decisions or determine their convictions? Do they do so with much thought? Discuss whether discipline should be used when so many other people are committing the same offense.

6

CHURCH DISCIPLINE:
PERSUADING TO REPENT

Church discipline begins when an offender has been exposed. This may happen in one of three ways. First of all, the offender may accuse himself. This is the situation in Matthew 5:23, 24, where the offender is instructed to go to the offended party and ask for forgiveness. The offender may be motivated to accuse himself if he knows that he has hurt the body of Christ and the name of Christ, even though his act is well hidden from public view. Alternatively, his offense may have become so well known that the magnitude of it has now pricked his conscience.

It is not self-accusation merely to talk (or even boast) about the episode(s) warranting discipline. Genuine self-accusation must be an act of confession directed toward repentance. It must be made in the spirit of making things right with God.

The second way in which an offender may be exposed is that the offended party brings an accusation against him. It is often very hard to step forward and accuse someone else. The accuser may be embarrassed by the circumstances of the sin or he may be afraid that his action will be interpreted as a vendetta (no matter how closely he is walking with the Lord). He may feel that the trauma of making an accusation would outweigh the benefits brought by discipline. Yet, he must do it. (Note the discussion in chapter 2 pertaining to Matthew 18:15–17.)

Finally, an offender may be exposed when his sin becomes common knowledge. This may happen, for example, when a divorce is obtained in the civil courts for reason of incompatibility.

Once an offender has been exposed, the elders are mandated to act. Their purpose must be to bring glory to God. This is accomplished when the offender repents, asks for forgiveness, makes restoration and is restored to full participation in the body (Gal. 6:1).

In the case of self-accusation, there is no need to determine if the offender is guilty. But in the other cases, the accused must be found guilty before judicial censure can be administered.

The elders begin the formal disciplinary process by issuing a citation to the accused person, asking him to appear before them. If he refuses to appear or leaves the church, a second request is issued. If he still chooses not to come, the elders must proceed to censure him. However, they will not proceed with a trial to determine if he is guilty; rather, they will censure him for his stubbornness, with the record indicating that an unresolved charge stands against him.

If an offender leaves the church when the charge has been lodged by self-accusation or is the result of common knowledge, the record must indicate not only that he has been censured for a specific offense (or offenses), but also that he has compounded his offense by refusing to appear and accept censure.

It is important that the elders understand the biblical meaning of repentance, since that is the essential first step leading to restoration. The verb "to repent" is often used in the New Testament to mean "to perceive afterwards" and "to change." Discipline is a tool in the hands of the Holy Spirit to change men—literally to change their direction 180 degrees. Repentance is a change of heart produced by the work of the Spirit. The Westminster Confession of Faith declares that "repentance unto life is an evangelical grace" (chap. 15, sect. 1). The prophecy of Zechariah 12:10 puts the concept into God's perspective: "And I will pour out on the house of David and the inhabitants of Jerusalem a spirit of grace and supplication. They will look on me, the one they have pierced, and they will mourn for him as one mourns for an only child, and grieve bitterly for him as one grieves for a firstborn son."

Repentance is part of our conversion. It is also called for by every sin we commit after we are converted. Paul stressed this: "I am afraid that when I come again my God will humble me before you, and I will be grieved over many who have sinned earlier and have not repented of the impurity, sexual sin and debauchery in which they have indulged" (2 Cor. 12:21).

Repentance starts with confession. David demonstrates: "Then I acknowledged my sin to you and did not cover up my iniquity. I said, 'I will confess my transgressions to the Lord'—and you forgave the guilt of my sin" (Ps. 32:5). Confession flows from the heart that "so grieves for, and hates his sins, as to turn from them all unto God, purposing and endeavoring to walk with him in all the ways of his commandments" (Westminster Confession of Faith, chap. 15, sect. 2).

Confession is coupled with a change of heart and conscience: "See what this godly sorrow has produced in you: what earnestness, what eagerness to clear yourselves, what indignation, what alarm, what longing, what concern, what readiness to see justice done" (2 Cor. 7:11).

A number of years ago a godly woman asked for help for her alcoholic husband. A Bible class was started in their home in the hope that the Lord would work through it to reclaim the husband. He attended sporadically. On occasion he would get drunk, wander off to some distant part of the country, and eventually call for help. The word of God was beginning to be used by the Spirit, but there was no real change that could be measured. Finally one day the husband confessed that he was a sinner. He had often admitted that he was wrong, pleaded for help, and made all kinds of protestations that he would change from that moment on. But when he confessed of his own volition that he was a sinner and had committed various particular sins, the Spirit of God changed his life. He eventually became an officer in the church.

Jeremiah 31:18, 19 describes the penitent heart. In its context the passage is captive Israel's corporate prayer of repentance, but it is also the prayer of every penitent heart: "You disciplined me like an unruly calf, and I have been disciplined. Restore me, and I will return, because you are the Lord my God. After I strayed, I repented; after I came to understand, I beat my breast. I was ashamed and humiliated because I bore the disgrace of my youth."

Psalm 51 further describes the heart of the penitent sinner. He is conscious—

- of danger before God—of being guilty (vss. 4, 9);
- of being polluted, of being ashamed and filled with self-loathing (vss. 5, 7, 10);
- of being helpless apart from God (vs. 11);
- that a disgraceful page of history has been written—by him (cf. "me" and "my" in vss. 1–3).

The apostle John gives the response of God's grace to three of these burdens of the heart. In 1 John 1:9 he declares that if we will confess our sin, there is forgiveness for the guilt ("He is faithful and just and will forgive us our sins"), cleansing from the pollution ("and purify us from all unrighteousness"), and power to overcome helplessness (by virtue of the promise being made in the first place). But, since the page of history remains, it is only by God's daily grace that the sinner can live with an abiding peace thereafter.

Confession to the offended party leads to a willingness to make a public confession. Only when the offender tells the body of his change of heart can reconciliation be completed and the body healed through his restoration. Galatians 6:1 sums it up: "Brothers, if someone is caught in a sin, you who are spiritual should restore him gently."

These are the component parts of repentance. These are the keys that unlock untold blessing for the penitent. They make it worthwhile to practice judicial discipline.

If repentance is not evident, the church must censure its member. The only censure that the church can administer is to withhold the means of blessing from the offender. The censure must be administered with two parameters in mind. First, the censure must not be more severe than the offense (cf. chapter 5). Second, the initial censure should normally not be severe; if the degree of severity is increased, it must be done in the context of love and gentleness, as well as firmness.

The various forms of censure, in increasing degrees of severity, are admonition, suspension, excommunication and deposition.

Admonition is a formal action taken by the elders (as opposed to the informal words of admonition provided by the support network). It is a reproof, warning the offender of guilt and danger and urging him to be more careful in the future.

Suspension is a directive that excludes the offender from participation in the sacraments. (A suspended church officer is excluded from his office during his suspension.) Although churches have not always listed it as a separate form of censure, suspension is specific enough to be treated as a separate step. If no evidence of repentance is forthcoming in a reasonable period of time, this censure should be changed to excommunication.

Occasionally a declaration of repentance is made by the

offender, but the honor of Christ's name demands that some public discipline be administered. In such cases suspension is imposed for a specified period of time. Wisdom must be used to determine the length of the suspension. Too long a period is unfair; too short a period will not do justice to the Lord's name.

If the offense is private in nature, the elders may choose not to rebuke the offender in public. But if it is public in nature (i.e., a heresy or immoral behavior that is not merely an individual matter), the elders would normally make a public announcement to the church.

Excommunication removes the offender from the church. It is the censure of last resort, and so should ordinarily be used only when there is gross immorality or heresy. It may sometimes be necessary to use it when an offender has aggravated a serious offense by stubbornly refusing to repent. Paul prescribed excommunication, knowing that an unrepentant sinner can be a hindrance to believers as they mature in Christ. In 1 Corinthians 5:4, 5 he states: "When you are assembled in the name of our Lord Jesus and I am with you in spirit, and the power of our Lord Jesus is present, hand this man over to Satan, so that the sinful nature may be destroyed and his spirit saved on the day of the Lord" (cf. 1 Tim. 1:20).

Notice that Paul teaches that even excommunication is intended to benefit the offender. If the offender is indeed a Christian, this will often shock him so traumatically that he will want to repent. And if he never was a genuine Christian, it will confirm his desperate need for the saving grace of God to work in his heart.

John Calvin points out an important distinction between excommunication and anathema (*Institutes*, book 4, chap. 12, sect. 10). It is the heretic who dies without repentance that is anathematized (cf. Acts 23:14; Rom. 9:3; Gal. 1:8, 9; 1 Cor. 12:3; 16:22). An anathema is God's declaration; the church should leave it to him.

Deposition (sometimes called defrocking) is a special censure for church officers. It removes the privilege of serving the church as an ordained person. It may be administered either separately or along with one of the censures discussed above.

When an offender repents, there is great blessing for him and for the church. Elders dare not ignore or excuse away the administration of discipline. Without it, not only is the blessing missed, but the offense often becomes a cancer in the body.

Questions for Reflection and Discussion

1. In what three ways may an offense be exposed?

2. In what ways is repentance expressed by a complete change of heart and life? Give illustrations of this. Explain how this is an act of God's grace.

3. Why is 1 John 1:9 so important to the experience of confession?

4. What are the three forms of censure for church members? List some of the benefits denied to the person by each censure.

7

THE BODY'S RESPONSE TO DISCIPLINE

While the censure of admonition or suspension is in effect, the offender is to be dealt with in firm yet loving ways. He should be reminded that the body of believers is hurting and that his own spiritual growth is suffering. The goal is his restoration. He should be urged to repent as the beginning of his restoration.

When the offender does repent and confess his sin, he must seek forgiveness and restoration. He must be concerned to see the body healed. And if anything can be done to make amends for his offense, such as returning stolen money, he must step forward and do it—however hard that may be for him.

Whenever someone confesses a personal offense involving more than two (or perhaps a few) people, the church must join in the expression of forgiveness: "Therefore, as God's chosen people, holy and dearly loved, clothe yourselves with compassion, kindness, humility, gentleness and patience. Bear with each other and forgive whatever grievances you may have against one another. Forgive as the Lord forgave you" (Col. 3:12, 13).

Paul emphasizes the necessity for such forgiveness in his comment to the church at Corinth: "The punishment inflicted on him by the majority is sufficient for him. Now instead, you ought to forgive and comfort him, so that he will not be overwhelmed by excessive sorrow" (2 Cor. 2:6, 7).

The response of forgiveness brings blessing and growth to the church. But forgiveness must be effectively communicated to the repentant person, or he may not share in the church's joy. Even so, it is hard to do.

In chapter 5 an illustration was given of an engineering student who had an immoral relationship with a young woman. When her parents learned of the situation, they were very hurt and became bitter. They made harsh statements to both young people. The young people confessed their sin, and asked them for forgiveness. They then proceeded to live quietly for the Lord for many years, all the while receiving abuse, until the Lord brought reconciliation.

In 2 Thessalonians 3:14, 15 Paul instructs the church to *shun* a certain individual (i.e., to institute a severe form of indefinite suspension). In doing so, he states two principles to guide the use of discipline. One instruction is that the elders (the judges) must not be prejudicial toward the offender, treating him as though he has been excommunicated. Even after he has been found guilty, he is not to be regarded as an enemy, but rather as a brother (vs. 15). The other instruction is that once a decision has been rendered, church members must continue to be deeply concerned for him (vs. 14).

The elders should normally do the following things to involve the congregation in the disciplinary action:

- Announce the censure.
- Indicate the seriousness of the offense. No specific details should ever be mentioned, although a reference to the type of offense (e.g., immorality, heresy or refusal to accept the oversight of the elders) may be in order.

- Call for prayer.

- Caution the members to refrain from any gossip.

- Warn the members to learn from this that Satan can and will attack any and all Christians, and therefore to be concerned with their own testimony and to be more dependent on the Lord.

These three additional things should be done in cases of excommunication:

- Announce that the offender is not welcome to participate in worship services until there is evidence of repentance.

- Instruct church members to be courteous to the offender, but not to enter into the typical experiences of Christian fellowship with him.

- State that the elders (in reliance upon the Holy Spirit) are primarily responsible to lead the offender to repentance, and that they are aggressively attempting to do so.

When excommunication is imposed, the church must follow Jesus' instructions to treat the offender "as you would a pagan or a tax collector" (Matt. 18:17). Paul adds: "With such a man do not even eat.... 'Expel the wicked man from among you'" (1 Cor. 5:11, 13). The key to these instructions is implied by the Lord in Matthew's gospel and is stated by Paul: "Hand this man over to Satan, *so that the sinful nature may be destroyed and his spirit saved on the day of the Lord*" (vs. 5, italics added). Paul gave the same message to Timothy about Hymenaeus and Alexander (1 Tim. 1:20).

It is true that we do not understand all that is involved in these verses. But we cannot escape the conclusion that a clear separation is made between the excommunicated party and the church. The elders in effect are saying to the offender: "You have claimed to be a Christian, but you are not acting like one.

Since you have not repented, and we can only judge the fruit of your life and not the intent of your heart, you must be removed from the body."

An announcement of censure should be made with great care. One procedure that has been used successfully is to announce on a Sunday morning that the next midweek service will be restricted to members of the church and that a disciplinary matter will be presented at that time for their prayer and concern.

All too often the church member who is faced with church discipline leaves the church. Sometimes he goes to another church; sometimes he just drops out of church life altogether. But when he does repent, great will be the joy in the church as well as in his heart!

When a suspended or excommunicated offender repents, he must profess his repentance before the offended party and the elders, and seek their forgiveness (2 Cor. 7:11–13). If the censure has been made public, he must also appear before the church. At that time the elders should declare publicly that he has been absolved from the censure previously imposed upon him. The removal of his censure must be recorded in the books of the church.

The removal of the censure of excommunication is more complicated and difficult than the removal of any other censure. This censure is so severe that the elders must be fully satisfied that the repentance is sincere—and not just remorse. This requires a lengthy period of observation after the offender has confessed, repented and made as much restoration as he can. This is especially true for an excommunicated minister (teaching elder).

The following outline indicates the steps to be taken after an excommunicated person has demonstrated true repentance:

A. For a former church member
   1. If the offender declares that he has only now become a Christian—
      a. remove the censure, with a public announcement as indicated above;
      b. enroll the individual in the usual class for candidates for membership;
      c. enroll him as a member by confession of faith.
   2. If the offender states that he has been a Christian all along—
      a. follow step (a) above;
      b. follow step (b) above;
      c. enroll him as a member by reaffirmation of faith;
      d. exhort, encourage and comfort him.
B. For a former minister (teaching elder)
   1. Make arrangements for the individual to be received into a church's membership (following the steps just given) immediately after the censure of excommunication has been removed.
   2. Have the individual make his confession before his former church court.
   3. Have his former church court determine what guidelines he must publicly commit himself to, governing—
      a. the conduct of his personal life;
      b. the exposing of his offense to any church before he accepts a position involving teaching or oversight of any kind.
   4. Remove the censure with a public announcement.
   5. Have the local congregation proceed to receive him into membership according to the steps given above for a repentant church member.

An assumption has been made throughout this discussion which must be stated clearly at this point. Everything in the disciplinary process must be bathed in prayer. This is of the utmost importance.

Questions for Reflection and Discussion

1. How can the lesson of 2 Corinthians 2:6, 7 be applied by a congregation seeking to demonstrate forgiveness?

2. What recommendations might be given to the congregation to guide the members when they meet someone who has been excommunicated? Refer to 1 Corinthians 5 and to 2 Thessalonians 3.

3. What does it mean that "the elders must be fully satisfied that the repentance is sincere—and not just remorse"?

8

ELDERS: SERVANT-LEADERS TO ADMINISTER DISCIPLINE

Elders administer church discipline. If they do not do so, much of their ministry will be counterproductive.

Elders must first of all be qualified for their office. As stated in 1 Timothy 3 and Titus 1, they are required to have Christ-like character and Christ-centered families. They must be committed to the doctrine and government of the church, and have a working knowledge of them. And they must have at least several basic gifts of the Spirit, along with some talents and skills. (Cf. *The Growing Local Church*, by Donald J. Mac-Nair [Grand Rapids: Baker Book House, 1975], p. 194). These qualifications must be confirmed in the men who are to serve as elders. This is accomplished in part by their election to office by the congregation.

A major implication of the election/confirmation process is that the members of the church perceive the elders to be wise and well qualified. That is, they are seen as men who learn from God's word and his works of providence. They must have the wisdom that only living through much of life's experiences can bring.

Wisdom can also be a direct gift of the Spirit. Paul speaks of "the message of wisdom" in 1 Corinthians 12:8. In 2:6–10 he indicates that the message is the gospel and that wisdom is the clarity of God's grace, as revealed by the Spirit. Wisdom is needed to make the gospel so clear and applicable that it cannot be missed.

Wisdom enables elders to see through a maze of details, which are often distorted by the involvement of the accuser and the accused, and get to the basic truth of the matter. The story of Solomon's wisdom in dealing with the two mothers and their babies demonstrates this point. The record concludes: "When all Israel heard the verdict the king had given, they held the king in awe, because they saw that he had wisdom from God to administer justice" (1 Kings 3:28).

As elders conduct their lives day by day, their wisdom is perceived by other church members. Also, the more they become part of the decision-making process of the church, the more their wisdom is sharpened and acknowledged. As a result, they gain the credibility that they will need when they must administer judicial discipline.

In order to be successful in administering church discipline, elders must not only have wisdom, but also must live by special standards. There are eight of these standards.

First, elders must be (and be perceived to be) servant-leaders. (Cf. *The Challenge of the Eldership*, by Donald J. MacNair [Philadelphia: Great Commission Publications, 1984], pp. 7–12.) They are called upon to be shepherds, guardians and administrators. (Cf. *The Living Church*, by Donald J. MacNair [Philadelphia: Great Commission Publications, 1980], pp. 64–67.) Serving well in these areas makes them more acceptable as judges.

Second, elders should serve as good examples. So should their families, since they will be watched by members of the congregation to some degree (living in the "fishbowl") except when they are by themselves.

Third, elders should be growing—and be perceived to be growing—in the fruit of the Spirit (Gal. 5:22, 23). Self-control is especially important, for Paul says: "Flee the evil desires of youth, and pursue righteousness, faith, love and peace, along with those who call on the Lord out of a pure heart. Don't have anything to do with foolish and stupid arguments, because you know they produce quarrels. And the Lord's servant must not quarrel; instead, he must be kind to everyone, able to teach, not resentful. Those who oppose him he must gently instruct, in the hope that God will grant them repentance leading them to a knowledge of the truth, and that they will come to their senses and escape from the trap of the devil, who has taken them captive to do his will" (2 Tim. 2:22–26). Two other qualities—love and patience—stand out as vital to the effective administering of discipline. The graces listed in the Galatians passage, in their perfection, describe Jesus. Elders should be growing to be like Christ, and the church must know it.

Fourth, elders should be constantly examining their own lives for unrepented sin. They must take the "plank" out of their own eyes (Matt. 7:3–5).

Fifth, elders must be willing to make hard decisions, however difficult or traumatic that may be. This implies that elders must be able to make decisions. When discipline is administered, no one can hide behind "consensus" decision making. Also, elders must be able to appreciate the possible consequences of their decisions and *still be willing to make them.* By doing so, they carry out their ordination vow to care for the flock entrusted to them (see *The Living Church,* pp. 43–45).

Sixth, elders must be ready to devote large blocks of time to disciplinary matters. Communication is a key part of the work, and that takes time. As Myron Rush points out, communication is not complete until understanding has been conveyed:

"Communication can be defined as *the process we go through to convey understanding from one person or group to another.* Unless understanding occurs, we have not communicated" (*Management: A Biblical Approach* [Wheaton, Ill.: Victor Books, 1983], p. 115). If insufficient time is provided, the "chemistry" of the Spirit's work in those involved may be destroyed.

Seventh, elders must exercise their faith by expecting God to work repentance in the heart of the offender. It is never enough simply to fulfill the letter of the law. Such discipline is really saying, "Let's get rid of the offender, but let's use a loophole to salve our consciences."

Elders will receive personal blessings from their ministry of discipline. There is the deep joy of being used by God. There is the blessing of seeing the entire body of Christ grow (individually and corporately) as the Spirit works in many hearts. Most of all, there is the blessing of knowing, no matter how difficult the work, that one's heart is right with God and that God is pleased with one's obedience.

Eighth, elders must accept a higher standard of accountability to God for their lives than is required of other church members. James declares: "Not many of you should presume to be teachers, my brothers, because you know that we who teach will be judged more strictly" (3:1). Accordingly, in the Presbyterian Church in America "a minister suspended or deposed for scandalous conduct shall not be restored, even on the deepest sorrow for his sin, until he shall exhibit for a considerable time such an eminently exemplary, humble and edifying life and testimony as shall heal the wound made by his scandal" (*The Book of Church Order*, §34–8).

There are two traps that elders fall into, which make it difficult, if not impossible, to administer church discipline. First, there is the problem of perception. Elders too often seem only to be carrying out the task of routine administration. They are then perceived to be little more than an executive committee making decisions involving administration and finance. Consequently, many members question whether elders have the credentials to administer judicial discipline.

In reply to a questionnaire answered by approximately 800 people, 82% of them indicated that they should feel confident to use the spiritual advice that their elders give them. And 65% indicated that they should be in submission to their elders as the best way to receive God's help and blessing. But only 29% indicated that they can easily get the ear of their elders to ask for advice. This situation can be changed. It must be changed for the best ministry of church discipline.

The second trap is discouragement, which Satan works overtime to produce in elders. "I don't measure up" and "It is too much for me" are the excuses most often made. But give God credit—he is still God! The Holy Spirit can and will strengthen each elder who humbly and earnestly seeks to walk with God. Weigh these matters, but live by faith.

Questions for Reflection and Discussion

1. How do the qualifications for eldership normally indicate that an elder has wisdom?

2. What are the eight standards which elders must follow if they are to administer church discipline effectively? Discuss at least two of them as they relate to being a leader.

3. What are the two traps that elders often fall into when administering church discipline? How is faith in the sovereignty of God fundamental to avoiding these traps?

9

PREPARATION FOR PROCEEDING WITH CHURCH DISCIPLINE

Elders dare not initiate or proceed with discipline without due preparation. This includes both personal and procedural matters.

They must share Christ's concern for his church in all areas of its life, including the area of discipline. His concern is expressed by his love for his own, both as individuals and as a body. As models of Christ, elders must express all aspects of this concern. Accordingly, the elders of the church should have the following convictions:

1. The church is the body of Christ in the world (Eph. 4:15, 16).

2. Since the body is made up of individuals, the elders must shepherd and guard them for their own sake and for the sake of the body's spiritual health. They must take seriously the teaching of 1 Corinthians 12:18—"But in fact God has arranged the parts in the body, every one of them, just as he wanted them to be."

3. It is the very name of Christ which is degraded by undisciplined sin.

4. Christ directs elders to administer discipline and will honor their obedient effort by blessing the process and vindicating his name.

5. The practice of discipline is not to be motivated by a desire to appease the offended party, vindicate his name, or defend the "good name" of the congregation in the community (2 Cor. 2 and 7).

Paul gives instructions that epitomize the concern that elders must demonstrate when administering discipline:

- "Do not repay anyone evil for evil" (Rom. 12:17).
- "If someone is caught in a sin, ... restore him gently" (Gal. 6:1; cf. 2 Cor. 2:7–11).
- "Do not be overcome by evil, but overcome evil with good" (Rom. 12:21).

Expressing this concern means using Christ's power. But the power that Christ gave to the church must be used for building up, and not for tearing down. Thus, Paul hoped "that when I come I may not have to be harsh in my use of authority—the authority the Lord gave me for building you up, not for tearing you down" (2 Cor. 13:10). Jesus declared this to be his attitude toward each of his own: "Come to me, all you who are weary and burdened, and I will give you rest. Take my yoke upon you and learn from me, for I am gentle and humble in heart, and you will find rest for your souls. For my yoke is easy and my burden is light" (Matt. 11:28–30).

If elders are motivated to administer discipline with any sense of revenge or without believing that God is working his will no matter what the outcome may be, they must appear before God in prayer and plead for forgiveness before sitting as judges. Their purpose can only be to be used by God according to his revealed word. Their hope must be that discipline will be used to bring repentance, restoration and a fruitful life to anyone convicted of an offense. Elders must seek the blessing for which Paul prayed: "And this is my prayer: that your love may abound more and more in knowledge and depth of insight, so that you may be able to discern what is best and may be pure and blameless until the day of Christ, filled with the fruit of righteousness that comes through Jesus Christ—to the glory and praise of God" (Phil. 1:9–11).

As discussed previously, elders are accountable to God for administering discipline (Heb. 13:17; cf. 2 Tim. 2:14; 4:2; Titus 2:15), and church members are to submit to their Christ-given authority (Heb. 13:17). The dynamics of authority and sub-mission demand of elders that scriptural safeguards be in place in their hearts. Elders, of all people, must be in submission to Christ as the Head of the church (Eph. 4:15) and the Lord of life (Col. 1:17, 18; 2 Cor. 5:10; Heb. 10:30). They, as much as any other church members, must be in submission to the will of Christ (2 Cor. 13:3, 4; Heb. 12:4–12) and the word of God (1 Tim. 4:11; Heb. 4:12).

The guidelines which govern procedure flow naturally from the elders' concern and sense of accountability.

Elders act as representatives of the Lord and exercise his authority. Unlike representatives in civil government, how-ever, they cannot make laws; they may only seek to have the re-vealed law of God enforced. Yet, as the Lord's representatives their judgments are binding.

Elders must be certain that everyone understands that they represent Christ, and therefore Christ's church. They must al-ways make it clear that there are really only two parties in a judicial case—the accused party and Christ's church. The church is represented by the prosecutor. The accuser, as part of the church, should be motivated only by a desire to vindicate the honor of Christ.

The elders must pursue only those charges which have the potential of being substantiated. Innuendos, generalities, gossip and guilt by association are improper grounds on which to bring charges. "'Every matter must be established by the testimony of two or three witnesses'" (2 Cor. 13:1, quoting Deut. 19:15). If this directive is not followed, there is not sufficient evidence on which to proceed.

Lest improper accusations be made, the elders must first warn the accuser that he may subject himself to judicial discipline if he makes a false accusation. Jesus declares: "Do not judge, or you too will be judged. For in the same way you judge others, you will be judged, and with the measure you use, it will be measured to you" (Matt. 7:1, 2).

Elders must proceed on the assumption that the accused person is innocent until proved guilty, even though they have been satisfied that there is sufficient evidence to press charges, have drawn up the charges, and have assumed the responsibility to sit as judges. If an elder cannot proceed on the presumption of innocence and judge with an open and fair mind, he must disqualify himself from sitting as a judge.

The elders must first be satisifed that the alleged offender is under their jurisdiction. They have no real authority over nonmembers. However, if an individual has for all intents and purposes become part of the body but has not joined the church, discipline may be in order for his good and for the health of the church.

The trouble with trying to discipline a nonmember is that there is no official way to process an accusation brought against him. Discipline can be attempted only if the nonmember accuses himself or if the offense is a matter of common knowledge. In these two situations the elders may try to censure a nonmember, but he will usually just leave the church, since he does not have a sense of submission to its authority and discipline.

Similarly, the elders of a local congregation may not

initiate or proceed with discipline against a minister who is a member and under the jurisdiction of a presbytery or similar regional church body. This would be true of most Presbyterian and Reformed denominations. The body of which he is a member is the court in which charges would have to be brought.

Elders must agree to the procedural details of the disciplinary process before proceeding with it. In most churches, procedures are already set forth in the rules of discipline to which elders swear agreement when they are ordained.

Elders must be sure that they do not practice partiality. Scripture teaches: "I charge you, in the sight of God and Christ Jesus and the elect angels, to keep these instructions without partiality, and to do nothing out of favoritism" (1 Tim. 5:21), and, "Do not pervert justice; do not show partiality to the poor or favoritism to the great, but judge your neighbor fairly" (Lev. 19:15).

Elders must act expeditiously. Satan is the one who gains when action is unduly delayed. It takes wisdom to know when an offender has been given sufficient time to repent. That time will be different in each situation. However, the biblical norm for personal anger indicates a model for the whole process of discipline: "'In your anger do not sin': Do not let the sun go down while you are still angry, and do not give the devil a foothold" (Eph. 4:26, 27).

As these guidelines indicate, elders need to understand the various parts of the trial before proceeding with it. Thus, elders who know little about the process of church discipline are well advised to seek mature guidance before and during their handling of a case. And even elders who understand the procedural details can benefit from the advice of a mature, experienced and trusted consultant. Such advice basically provides three things: (1) detailed knowledge of the proper procedures to be followed, (2) creative insights to help think through the situation, and (3) safeguards to keep the work in order.

Proper attitude, preparation and attention to the guidelines will pay rich dividends. Together they will help to insure that discipline is properly administered.

Questions for Reflection and Discussion

1. 1 Timothy 4:12 indicates that elders are to be examples. Why does such modeling of Christ include demonstrating a concern for discipline? How should elders demonstate such concern in everyday life, apart from cases of church discipline?

2. How do Romans 12:17, Galatians 6:1 and Romans 12:21 govern the elders' administration of discipline?

3. How must elders be in submission, even as they stand accountable over others before the living God?

4. What procedural guidelines govern the administration of church discipline? Discuss how any two of them come into play when an accusation is brought against a member.

10

BIBLICAL ATTITUDES ABOUT "MY DAY IN COURT"

"My day in court!" The availability of judicial process provides the ultimate assurance to each individual that justice will be done. Both the civil and the ecclesiastical courts make provision for it.

However, it is not easy to go through a church trial. When a trial is conducted to determine guilt or innocence, enormous spiritual and emotional trauma is involved. The individuals involved, their families, the local church, the denomination and the Christian community at large are all affected. The impact can be much greater than that produced by a civil trial, for many more people are usually directly touched by it.

The "glue" that holds a congregation together is the unity and strength that come from the network of believers supporting each other. A trial that threatens any part of the network is a threat to all the members of it, and thus to the unity and possibly even to the life of the network itself. A trial also affects Christians in general, for they are "tarred with the same brush" of criticism because of it.

Therefore, church trials should be avoided unless they are necessary. One must carefully consider both the instructions of Scripture and the "trauma factor" of a trial. This advice should not to be construed as ruling out church trials. But the *only* church trials should be those that are necessary and proper.

There are several rules which can help to determine whether a trial should really be conducted. They also indicate what attitude to have about conducting one.

Rule #1: Work and pray with all diligence to avoid taking the final step that turns a charge into an indictment and thereby mandates a church trial.

Several attitudes that are all too common can lead to a hasty decision to conduct a church trial. By identifying them it is often possible to avoid an undesirable trial. Some (especially those who have not matured a great deal, but have a thorough knowledge of doctrine and church government) think first in terms of a trial rather than in terms of pastoral ministry to clear up a situation. They believe that a trial is the best way, and possibly the only way, to vindicate the name of the Lord. They often think of the potential trial in black-and-white terms and do not fully appreciate the heartache of the human lives involved.

Another counterproductive attitude surfaces especially when the charge has to do with heresy. Men can become so involved with their own precise articulation of a doctrine that they fail to understand each other when discussing the issue. This problem is sometimes aggravated by a personality conflict. This can lead (sometimes at Satan's bidding) to a cry for a "trial" to resolve the conflict.

These circumstances can be controlled to a large extent by calling upon men of God to help find a solution. These men should be servant-leaders who are respected by all the parties involved. They should be men of prayer and spiritual maturity. They should be seen to exercise wisdom in their lives—wisdom based on a comprehensive knowledge of the Bible and a significant amount of practical experience. Such men of God would, of course, agree to the limitations of authority under which they would serve and to the lines of communication they would follow. The agreements would be made before they begin to help.

Rule #2: Do not even consider having a trial when the subject at issue divides the respected authorities in one's theological tradition.

This rule seems so obvious that one wonders why anyone would do anything else. But some men do ignore it once they have come to a firm conviction about a subject and have found leading authorities who share their opinion. Then, they fail to search far enough to find other opinions or they ignore or discount them. The truth is that they have not done their homework.

It is sometimes thought that a trial dealing with statements that seem to go beyond the limits of interpretation allowed by the church is the way for the church to define those limits more clearly. This would supposedly demonstrate that the church is very serious about maintaining its purity of doctrine. However, one cannot expect a church trial to produce clearly defined truth, for it does not provide the right setting for the necessary deliberations. It is true that the accused should prepare a well-supported doctrinal statement for consideration by the court (preferably distributed beforehand). But ordinarily it would only be a background paper, not the main document in the case.

The accused usually puts forward his defense in order to clear his name, to encourage his family, and to maintain his ministry. He must deal with the exact wording of the indictment and demonstrate that the charge is not true. Therefore, his defense would probably not be developed around an exhaustive explanation of his doctrinal position. He may well be prepared to argue the overall doctrinal issue, but such argumentation would seldom be the best way to defend his innocence in the matter.

Note, too, that such a charge almost automatically carries with it the additional charge of disturbing the peace and unity of the church and undermining its purity. This makes it even more necessary to address the specific charges in the indictment, not abstract doctrinal questions. Thus, the final result of the trial will not be a definitive declaration of the precise limits of the doctrine in question.

Furthermore, even if the accused chooses to present a fully developed doctrinal statement as the basis for his defense, the court will reach its verdict (if it finds no other cause for guilt) only by deciding between the theological positions presented to it by the two sides. And no matter what it decides, its decision will have to enjoy wide support over a considerable length of time before it becomes the accepted doctrinal interpretation of the entire church.

The chart on the opposite page indicates which charges should be processed into indictments and which should be settled by pastoral care.

Rule #3: Careful consideration must be given to "people involvement" before issuing an indictment.

The mere fact that many people know about an issue (and are bewildered and probably hurt by it) does not in itself mean that a trial should be avoided or aborted. But, it does call for careful consideration before conducting one.

There are two sets of criteria to consider before processing a charge. The first set deals with the party (or parties) offended. If the offense is committed against an individual, it is a *personal* offense. In such a case Matthew 18:15–18 must be followed step by step before any charge can be brought. Often the problem will be resolved before a trial becomes necessary.

WHEN TO PROCESS A CHARGE INTO AN INDICTMENT

Assumption #1: The alleged offender has denied sinning.

Assumption #2: All parties are committed to the same system of doctrine and government.

The Charge (well documented when necessary)	Whether an Indictment Should Be Issued
Immorality Contradicting church doctrine Breaking ordination vows	Must
Consistently appearing to contradict church doctrine Consistently appearing to break ordination vows	Probably
Consistently going beyond the limits of interpretation allowed by the church [1] Usurping leadership [2] Actions unbecoming of a Christian [3]	Possibly
Making statements about doctrine that are within the limits of interpretation allowed by the church Misusing leadership [4]	Never

NOTES

[1] In the light of rule #2, this offense would not normally be the grounds for an indictment.

[2] Since it is almost impossible to prove improper motivation, this charge should not normally be used. But the charge of assuming authority over the spiritual lives of others without the church having bestowed that authority by way of election and ordination to office might well be provable.

[3] If there is immoral activity involved, it would be dealt with in the first category. If the accused is charged with exercising poor or immature judgment (no matter how bad the judgment is or how much trouble it caused), a trial would not normally be appropriate. But the circumstances might justify an indictment in the case of an ordained church officer.

[4] Same as [3], except that the last sentence does not apply.

Sometimes, however, the offended party will conclude that the offense is not such that the well-being of the church would ever be threatened by it. In such a case he may ask the alleged offender for the sake of Christ's honor not even to give the appearance of offending again, and then drop the charge. Or, the offended party in this circumstance may simply "leave it with the Lord" and drop the charge. The elders may promote such a solution and commit themselves to continue in prayer for and with all the parties involved.

If the offense is not committed against a particular individual, it is a *general* offense. In such a case there is little doubt that a trial is necessary if the sin is not admitted.

The second set of criteria deals with how many people know about the sin. If only a few people know about it, it is a *private* offense. This type of offense may often be dealt with as if it were a personal offense. However, if many people know about it, it is a *public* offense. Since it is common knowledge, it requires a trial if there is no admission of guilt. Again, it is best to avoid having a trial if that is at all possible.

Rule #4: A trial ultimately has no winners.

The indictment is always brought by the church of Jesus Christ against the accused, never by the accuser against the accused. Church discipline should never be used to vindicate or placate an individual. The honor of the Lord's name is all that is at stake.

However, there is still a human element involved as soon as a trial is instituted. The prosecution seeks to vindicate the name of the Lord; the defense seeks to maintain that the Lord's name has not been shamed and therefore that the accused is innocent. If a verdict of guilty is reached, the prosecutor gets a sense of achievement—he feels like a "winner." And the defendant feels like the "loser." The feelings are of course reversed if the accused is found not guilty.

Since so much distress and grief will result from the

disruption and publicity of a church trial, everyone should try to avoid having a trial in the first place. If it is unavoidable, it must be conducted with heavy hearts. It might serve the Lord well not only to begin a trial by reading Galatians 6:1 ("Brothers, if someone is caught in a sin, you who are spiritual should restore him gently") and confessing the church's grief before the Lord, but also to interrupt the trial on occasion to remind everyone of these things.

Rule #5: The peace, purity and unity of the body must be given the highest priority when there is the possibility of avoiding a trial. There are some circumstances in which there is no option but to have a trial; this rule applies to all other situations.

Sometimes the accuser believes that the glory of the Lord demands a trial, but the congregation does not even suspect that a problem exists. If his accusation provides only probable cause for proceeding with an indictment, and especially if it provides only possible cause for proceeding, it is usually best for him to defer to the well-being of the body and not demand a trial. This might mean that the accuser would have to leave the church or even give up the pastorate (if he is the pastor). On the surface this appears to be running away from a problem rather than facing it. In reality, however, it is a decision calling for great spiritual maturity and sacrifice.

Rule #6: Public media should be respected, but not given opinions about a trial.

The church has nothing to hide when conducting a trial. Reporters should be permitted into the courtroom. They should be given a carefully prepared background briefing so that they will be able to understand the indictment and the court proceedings. During the trial a designated officer of the court should be available to the press in order to answer questions, offer explanations, and generally be of assistance (providing telephones, etc.).

No arbitrary rule should be made to bar the press from the

trial. That would only inflame both the atmosphere of the trial and any reports the press might issue. It might also infringe the civil rights of some of the individuals involved. On the other hand, all members of the court (and everyone else in the church, for that matter) should politely decline to give their opinion of the trial to anyone in the media. And the court should probably decide on its verdict in private.

These six rules simply apply common sense to the concept of a church trial. They may help to avoid unnecessary trials. They should be thought through with great care and be used whenever a trial is a possibility.

Questions for Reflection and Discussion

1. Why do some ministers apparently rush into church trials too quickly?

2. What are the differences between the charges that are described in the chart entitled "When to Process a Charge into an Indictment"?

3. How important to the decision to issue an indictment is the fact that the offense is well known?

4. Why is it that a trial ultimately has no winners?

11

STEP BY STEP THROUGH
A CHURCH TRIAL

The elders are normally referred to as the "court" and as "judges" while they are handling a case. This may sound threatening, at least at first. But member and elder alike should remember that the very words of Jesus in Matthew 18 demand that the church "govern its members even to the extent of disciplinary measures when these become necessary" (*Biblical Church Discipline,* by Daniel E. Wray [Carlisle, Pa.: The Banner of Truth Trust, 1978], p. 3).

Elders must resist two opposing temptations at this point. On the one hand, they must not shrink back from carrying out their responsibility to judge church members. On the other hand, they must not act without personal submission to Christ or in order to gratify a sinful desire to lord it over people.

When the elders set themselves up as a court, they establish the proper context within which to proceed with the charge before them. By doing so, they commit themselves to act with decorum, impartiality and great care.

The elders should not constitute themselves a court unless

there is strong evidence of guilt. As pointed out in chapter 6, such evidence can come before them through self-accusation, an accusation made by an offended party, or common knowledge. They do not have such evidence simply because they have received a charge against someone or because they feel something is wrong. In either case the elders must first try to resolve the apparent problem pastorally.

If an accuser charges that he has been personally sinned against, the elders must first be sure that he has diligently and earnestly followed the instructions of Jesus in Matthew 18:15, 16. They may not go any further in the process until this has been done. It does not matter how long this takes, although they should require prompt compliance from the accuser.

Once the accuser has confronted the offender and is still not satisfied that there has been a resolution of the problem, he must take one or two witnesses with him and again seek a resolution. The best witnesses are people who themselves have knowledge of the alleged offense. But if the offended party does not know of such people, his witnesses should be people who could help to resolve the problem or, if necessary, testify to the sincerity and completeness with which the instructions in Matthew 18 have been carried out.

Elders may, of course, be those witnesses. However, many times it is wiser to use mature Christians who are not elders. For instance, if the confrontation is between two women, it would often be prudent to have women serve as the witnesses.

If there is still no resolution, the offended person should bring his charge before the elders. The elders, *serving as shepherds*, should then visit the accused and determine whether there is a satisfactory explanation or strong presumption of guilt. This must be done with care and discretion, but very diligently. The entire effort must be bathed in prayer.

If the elders are satisfied with the explanation given by

the accused, they must see to it that all the parties are fully reconciled and that the matter is finally settled.

If the offender admits his guilt and repents of his sin, the elders will have to decide how to deal with the matter so as best to bring glory to God. In such an instance there is no need for the elders to constitute themselves a court.

If the elders see that there is strong presumption of guilt, they should plead with the accused to confess his sin before the Lord. If this happens, the elders will only have to deal with a self-accused individual, which will not require a formal trial. But if he does not confess, the elders must decide if they should proceed to constitute themselves a court.

In the case of the self-accused person, the court proceeds directly to determine the censure to be imposed. No formal trial is necessary.

In all cases of alleged heresy, the court should require the accused to prepare a paper that states his position, supported by biblical and other documentation. It is understood that this documentation will be used as evidence if the case is brought to trial.

In all cases that are to go to trial, the court must appoint a prosecutor to conduct the case against the accused. Normally he is a member of the court, although he may simply be a member of the congregation. It is unwise (and illegal in some churches) to use professional lawyers either as the prosecutor or the defense lawyer. The prosecutor's first responsibility is to prepare an indictment, which should specify the offenses and the basis for court action. He must give a copy of the indictment and a list of witnesses to the accused. He must also issue a citation to each party in the case—the accused, the accuser(s) and the witnesses—to appear before the court at its next session. The indictment should state the times, places and circumstances set by the court.

The accused should appoint a defense lawyer to represent him in court. His lawyer should prepare for the trial by gathering evidence and subpoenaing witnesses, meeting with the moderator and the prosecutor to discuss procedures to be followed and evidence to be presented, and formulating a plan of defense.

Care should be taken to satisfy the guidelines discussed in chapter 9. In this regard the accuser is always the church, since the church is the injured party. The prosecutor acts on behalf of the church.

Once the court is constituted, a presiding judge must be chosen. His first action should be to admonish the court as to the seriousness of the situation and remind them of the responsibility that the apostle Paul places on them: "Brothers, if someone is caught in a sin, you who are spiritual should restore him gently. But watch yourself, or you also may be tempted" (Gal. 6:1); and, "I charge you, in the sight of God and Christ Jesus and the elect angels, to keep these instructions without partiality, and to do nothing out of favoritism" (1 Tim. 5: 21).

The court next should determine whether a judicial committee (made up of members of the court) needs to be established. Its function would be to prepare a summary of all the papers, arrange them for presentation, and determine the order in which the court should handle the various aspects of the case. Such a committee is highly recommended.

Before proceeding, the court must determine that the citations have been served.

At the next (second) meeting of the court, the charges are read to the accused, and he is asked to plead guilty or not guilty. If the accused does not appear, he shall be cited a second time and warned that presumptive action will be taken by the court if he still refuses to appear.

Witnesses are essential to trying the case. Here are a few rules that govern their testimony:

- A witness must be competent to testify.
- A husband or a wife cannot be compelled to testify against the other.
- The testimony of more than one witness, or the testimony of one witness plus corroborative evidence properly certified and presented, is needed in order to substantiate a charge.
- Each witness must commit himself by oath or affirmation to tell the full truth, to the best of his ability.
- Witnesses must be examined in the presence of the accused.

When the trial begins, these steps shall be followed:

- The witnesses called by the prosecution shall be examined by the prosecutor, cross-examined by the defense counsel, and finally reexamined by the prosecutor.
- The witnesses called by the defense shall be similarly examined, cross-examined, and reexamined.
- The prosecutor shall present a summation of his case, including the evidence that substantiates the charge.
- The defense counsel shall be heard in the same way.
- The prosecutor shall close his case.
- The members of the court shall express their opinions.
- The court shall vote by roll call, a majority vote being decisive.
- The verdict shall be announced.
- The judgment shall be entered upon the books and announced to all the parties.

The members of the court may ask for explanations or clarification at any time. However, they may not develop additional evidence. The defense counsel and the prosecutor may address questions to the court at any time. If the court chooses to introduce these questions, it may.

From beginning to end the proceedings are to be bathed in prayer.

No attempt has been made in this discussion to deal with organizational details (e.g., the number of days between the serving of the indictment and the beginning of the trial), the possibility of appealing a decision, the conditions under which elders must disqualify themselves from membership on the court, offenses that took place well before the charge was placed, etc. These matters are dealt with in most churches' rules of discipline. If rules governing these matters are not already in place, they must be established before the court is constituted.

Questions for Reflection and Discussion

1. Why is it necessary for the elders to make a specific decision to constitute themselves a court?

2. Why should the elders deal with a charge pastorally before arranging for a trial? How should they carry out this responsibility?

3. What are the responsibilities of the prosecutor? What instructions and information should he give when summoning the parties in the case?

4. Why should the presiding judge call Galatians 6:1 and 1 Timothy 5:21 to the attention of the court before it proceeds with its work?

5. What are the implications of examining witnesses in the presence of the accused?

12

GETTING DISCIPLINE STARTED IN AN ESTABLISHED CHURCH

Experience shows that Satan is vicious in his attack on an infant congregation. He does not wait until it has grown in strength and unity. He attacks when it is embryonic. Discipline will probably be needed within the first six months of its life in order for the church to weather Satan's attack.

Yet, if the church is taught from the beginning that discipline is part of its fabric, it will not be too difficult to have it accepted. At first it may not be much more than an academic discussion, but the foundation will have been laid.

It is much harder to introduce church discipline into a congregation that is already well established. This is shown by the situations in 1 Corinthians 5 and in 2 Thessalonians 2. In an established church, discipline is introduced for one of two reasons. First, gross sin or heresy may have developed and become common knowledge. Or, the leadership of the church, recognizing that discipline is part of a healthy church, may want to have it well established before any problem develops.

If the elders find that they must proceed with a disciplinary case and the church is not prepared for it, there are five steps to follow:

1. Prayer support should be immediately established for the parties involved, for the church, and for the elders, who will need wisdom and fortitude as they deal with the problem. The situation will dictate whether or not the entire congregation should be involved with this prayer support.

2. A mature, objective person should almost always be sought out for consultation. He will, in effect, be a teacher and a facilitator. He should be recognized as trustworthy, since he will become privy to the entire situation. He should be spiritually mature, have some experience with church discipline, and know how church government works.

3. Then, the elders must take a "crash course" in church discipline as soon as possible. This should be done *before* they become deeply involved with the details of the situation. The consultant will teach the course, if possible. As they undertake this study, the elders must recognize that their lack of knowledge about church discipline is not a sufficient reason to evade the present situation. They must also recognize that God will use their proper exercise of church discipline to bring glory to his name. They should also be committed to developing and adopting long-range plans to institute the proper practice of church discipline in the future.

4. The elders must prepare a set of steps (including a timetable) to guide them as they proceed with the case. It should be recognized from the beginning that these steps will be subject to constant revision. They should include ways to evaluate the process as it goes forward. Feedback should be utilized during the process.

5. Once plans are in place, the process begins.

When elders recognize the need to integrate church discipline into the fabric of the church, even though no particular case needs to be dealt with, the task is less difficult—but just as necessary. Here are the steps to follow:

1. Prayer support should be set up for the elders and for the program. It should involve the elders, the deacons and other leaders, and the corporate prayer of the congregation.

2. Through the pastor's sermons and in other ways, the congregation should be taught the doctrine of the church. Church discipline should be emphasized, but it must be put in the proper context.

3. The elders should work through the concepts and the details of church discipline at a daylong retreat. A major goal of the retreat should be to get a commitment from each elder to support the use of church discipline. The elders should be prepared to think through the proposals for practicing church discipline. Each should be asked to accept the proposals on a provisional basis, to think and pray about them, and to consider adopting them in the near future.

At this retreat, the following proposals should be introduced:

a. If the church does not have an active support network, plans should be made to develop one.

b. The congregation's perception of the elders as servant-leaders should be strengthened by:

- enhancing appreciation of what servant-leadership is,
- conducting a self-evaluation (or obtaining professional evaluation) of one's servant-leadership performance, and
- serving the members more directly as shepherds.

c. Consideration should be given to emphasizing confession in corporate worship.

d. Efforts should be made to insure that church members fully appreciate the scriptural requirement that they live holy lives. This can be done by:

- appealing to them to be sensitive to the work of God (1 Cor. 1:10; 10:31; 2 Cor. 10:1, 2; Gal. 4:12; Phil. 4:9),
- admonitioning them to avoid the need for discipline (1 Cor. 6:13-15, 19, 20; 11:20–22; 14:3; 2 Cor. 5:7, 11; Phil. 2:12, 13; 3:16; 1 Thess. 2:12; 4:1; 5:12; 1 Tim. 3:14, 15), and
- identifying the commands in Scripture to avoid sin (2 Thess. 3:6; 1 Tim. 1:3; 4:11; 6:17, 18).

e. When new members are oriented, they should be taught the concepts of church discipline. Great care should be given to the context and manner in which it is taught.

f. Thorough training in church discipline should be included in future officer training programs.

g. The church's bylaws should be amended as necessary.

4. At the next elders' meeting, the proposals should be acted upon. Target dates (probably spread over a two-year period) should be adopted for implementing them. A program of evaluation and feedback must be included.

5. The proposals adopted by the elders should be reported to the congregation.

6. Church groups should be organized to discuss the concepts of discipline and the elders' report. The purpose of these groups would be to promote understanding and provide an opportunity for feedback.

7. The elders should study the responses from the discussion groups and refine their report if necessary.

8. The elders should visit the families of the church in order to answer questions and foster understanding. They must dispel any fear that they are developing a "control syndrome." They must be perceived as leading the church into greater conformity to the New Testament model of the church and seeking to develop greater love and unity in the body.

9. The program should be formally introduced into the life of the church. If any bylaws need to be amended, this must be done.

Church discipline is natural in a healthy church—hard, but natural.

Questions for Reflection and Discussion

1. What are the two reasons why church discipline is finally introduced into an established church? Why is it harder to get it started in such a church than it would have been at its beginning?

2. When discipline is being introduced in an established church because of a gross sin or heresy, what should be the attitude of the elders as they study the concepts of church discipline? Why?

3. In the long-range plans to introduce church discipline into an established church, emphasis should be placed on corporate confession during church worship. What goal will be accomplished by this?

4. Why should the elders visit the families of the church while a program of church discipline is being introduced?

13

CHURCH DISCIPLINE AND CIVIL LAW

"Anyone can be sued. The Christian must be sure that he is being sued for righteousness' sake." This quote from a Christian lawyer puts the subject into focus.

Since the church is in the world but not of the world (John 17:14, 15), it must live in tension with the world and its governments. The Bible makes plain what the attitude of the church and its members must be, both to Christ and to the world—whatever the resulting tension may be.

Scripture declares that the church is to be subject to Christ and his law: "He is before all things, and in him all things hold together. And he is the head of the body, the church; he is the beginning and the firstborn from among the dead, so that in everything he might have the supremacy" (Col. 1:17, 18).

Christians in the Western world, even in the United States, must recognize that their allegiance to Christ is shared by only a minority of the population. Until the 1960s and 1970s, many American Christians believed that most people in their communities and country accepted and followed Christian values. Actually, however, Christian values are not very influential in contemporary society. The prevailing culture is not sympathetic to them.

Scripture also declares that Christians are to be subject to the state: "Everyone must submit himself to the governing authorities, for there is no authority except that which God has established.... Therefore, it is necessary to submit to the authorities, not only because of possible punishment but also because of conscience" (Rom. 13:1, 5). When tension arises between the demands of Christ and the demands of the world, Christians have this instruction: "Dear friends, I urge you, as aliens and strangers in the world, to abstain from sinful desires, which war against your soul. Live such good lives among the pagans that, though they accuse you of doing wrong, they may see your good deeds and glorify God on the day he visits us" (1 Pet. 2:11, 12).

The Bible is the final authority for applying these principles. The eternal principles (the absolutes) which it reveals must be the standards by which Christians structure their decisions and actions. Rather than shrink back from living by absolutes in a society moving contrary to them, the church must be both thankful and filled with awe that God has made it "the pillar and foundation of the truth" (1 Tim. 3:15). The church is the resource for truth in a lost, humanistic and materialistic world.

If the church is to maintain God's truth as the answer to man's needs, it must practice that truth. Therefore, it must practice church discipline. When church discipline is exercised with an awareness of civil law and civil rights, it can often be administered without consequent civil suits. But, whether the offender is submissive or rebellious, the church may not ignore unrepented sin.

Unrepentant offenders smart under discipline. The church can therefore expect civil suits from them, or worse. It must remember that "the message of the cross is foolishness to those who are perishing" (1 Cor. 1:18), and this attitude of the unsaved is often that of the offending church member.

However, the church can avoid lawsuits (or at least have them dismissed) by carefully living within the laws of the land. This can ordinarily be done without disobeying Christ. Church officers have the scriptural mandate to "direct the affairs of the church *well*" (1 Tim. 5:17, italics added), and so they must attempt to protect Christ's body in this way. This means both protecting the authority of the church as a civil entity and protecting the civil rights of those involved in church discipline.

The Plymouth Rock Foundation of Marlborough, N.H., in its "FAC-Sheet #19," makes this statement about Old Testatment justice, which provides the context within which guidelines relating church discipline to civil law may be developed:

> All justice was to be based on righteous judgements *(Deut 25:1; Ps 82)*. The corruption of justice is an abomination to The Lord *(Pr 17:15)* and perverted justice is not justice but is against God's will *(Isa 59:14)*. Justice is to be meted out equally, and even-handedly; no man is above the law, no man is beneath the law *(Deut 1:16, 17; John 7:24)*.
>
> In God's eyes, justice is *synonymous* with righteousness; where there is no righteousness, there is no justice.

The courts of today may not fully live up to this standard. But Christians are bound by the word of God to work towards court systems that reasonably achieve it. The more it is achieved, the greater will be the legal protection afforded to the church to carry out its legitimate functions.

The church is to live in such a way that if it is sued in civil court, it is being sued for righteousness' sake. It dare not find itself being sued because it has violated its biblical standards regarding the rights and responsibilities of its members, or because it has been too lazy or calloused to be concerned about them. By the same token, the church must not be so afraid of civil suits that it is unwilling or unable to proceed with church discipline when it is needed.

Questions for Reflection and Discussion

1. How does 1 Peter 2:11, 12 help the Christian as he faces the tension between the church of Jesus Christ and the world with its courts?

2. Why does maintaining the truth demand the practicing of it?

14

GUIDELINES RELATING CHURCH DISCIPLINE TO CIVIL LAW

Elders should enjoy the confidence that they have properly done all that is necessary to protect both the authority of the church as a civil entity and the civil rights of its members as citizens. This means that they have done what is necessary, and have neither neglected their responsibilities nor misused their authority. It also implies that they have not gone overboard in "busyness" work in their attempt to be complete and accurate.

Elders can enjoy this confidence if they follow the guidelines given in this chapter. Explanatory information is also provided in order to introduce these guidelines and show how to use them effectively.

The case of Marian Guinn, which may well become a landmark case heard by the Supreme Court of the United States, illustrates the need for guidelines relating church discipline to civil law. The facts of this case will now be presented without comment or judgment.

Marian Guinn sued the Collinsville (Oklahoma) Church of

Christ for "invasion of privacy" and "extreme and outrageous" conduct that caused her severe emotional distress. She argued that the disciplinary action taken against her and the way in which it was done were both wrong. The church officers had told her (quite often) that she was living in sin and needed to repent. On September 21, 1981, they wrote to her, warning that they would "tell it to the church" (Matt. 18:17) unless she repented. On September 24 she wrote a letter of resignation. She stated that whatever had been discussed was a private matter, and that she did not want her name mentioned publicly. A few days later the congregation was informed. The members were asked to contact her about her need and were told that she had a week in which to repent (by October 4). On October 5 the congregation was read the Scriptures which the officers believed she had broken. Her name was removed from the roll. A letter about this was sent to the congregation and to several nearby churches in the same denomination.

The officers of this church would have been helped by guidelines relating church discipline to civil law. Here are eleven such guidelines:

Guideline #1: *Develop a working relationship with legal counsel.* In many cases there should be a professional relationship involving a regular retainer fee. In every new situation get advice concerning the application of civil law to the protection of both the authority of the church and the civil rights of its members. Help is available from the Christian Legal Society, P. O. Box 2069, Oak Park, Illinois 60303.

Guideline #2: *Teach candidates for church membership (and church members, too) that the vows taken when joining the church are very serious.* The church requires its members to submit themselves to the oversight of the elders, and they vow to do so. The Westminster Confession of Faith states that vows bind "to performance, although to a man's hurt" (chap. 22, sect. 4).

Dr. J. Carl Laney, associate professor of biblical literature at Western Conservative Baptist Seminary, suggests that a statement like this be included in the church constitution: "We the members of First Church will not pursue legal action or sue the pastors, elders, deacons, or church staff in connection with the performance of their official duties" ("Church Discipline Without a Lawsuit," *Christianity Today*, November 9, 1984, p. 76). Such a statement would reinforce the vows required for church membership.

Guideline #3: *Be sure that the legal documents of the church are clear, accurate and complete.* There usually are three such documents: the constitution, the bylaws and the charter of incorporation. The constitution "is primarily a document of principles which are the foundation upon which the church life and its operation are structured and which are not expected to change" (*The Birth, Care, and Feeding of a Local Church*, by Donald J. MacNair [Grand Rapids: Baker Book House, 1971], p. 124). The set of bylaws "is primarily a document of implementation of the principles enunciated in the constitution. Therefore, it must be flexible, reflecting the changes occurring in the church from its growth and increased outreach" (ibid.). The content of the charter of incorporation ("trusteeship" in some states) depends on the laws of the state. Sometimes the constitution and bylaws are submitted as the charter.

The constitution of a denominational church usually consists of the doctrinal standards of the denomination, its book of government and discipline, and sometimes its book of worship. If so, the officers of the church must bind themselves to uphold that system of doctrine and government and be reasonably adept at working with them.

In nondenominational churches the officers must be satisfied that the constitution of their church is clear, accurate and complete. They should review it annually and update it as necessary.

The bylaws, although mostly concerned with procedural details, cannot be taken for granted. If the seemingly minor rules regulating church discipline are ignored or misused, a disgruntled member may, when censured, base a civil suit upon such misconduct. In Georgia and other states religious societies are free to follow their own rules with respect to the expulsion of members, but where there are no such rules, a member must be given notice and an opportunity to defend himself before he can be expelled. (Consult legal counsel to determine what the law is in your own state.)

The charter of incorporation sets up the church as a corporation under state law. A corporation is governed by a board of directors or trustees, whose function should be clearly stated in the charter. Be sure that the actual work of the trustees is in accord with the document. If the church trustees are set up as a board of directors, they have the legal authority (and obligation) to run the church. But if their function is simply to hold the church property in trust for its members, their authority is much more limited, as stated in the charter.

Misunderstanding and misuse of the charter almost always cause friction between members and officers as to the use, development or ownership of property. The tension may result in disciplinary action and/or lawsuits over control of the property and over the terms of the discipline.

Care must be taken to interpret and apply the church documents properly. During the heat of dispute or discipline, church officers may forget their commitment to principles and disregard or circumvent predetermined procedures. But to do so is to invite a lawsuit.

Guideline #4: *Teach the biblical meaning of officer account-ability and member submission.* Two groups with whom this should regularly be done are the young people and candidates for membership. This should also be dealt with in the preaching ministry of the pastor. Adult classes should occasionally study the subject.

Whenever a special situation arises in the church or is reported in the media, it should be reviewed by the elders.

They should occasionally set up a forum in which they can lead the members in a discussion of the issue while it is still a topic of general interest. For instance, most American churches have members who are aware of the Marian Guinn case because of media coverage. The publicity should have created an occasion for the teaching, preaching and discussion of church discipline.

Guideline #5: *When new members join the church, call upon them to submit themselves to the authority of the elders.* This commitment must be based on the member's sense of responsibility for the health of the entire body of believers (1 Cor. 12:18). There should even be instructions on why, how and when a resignation may be submitted to the church, or at least a guide should be available to the member who may choose to resign.

Guideline #6: *Teach the subject of church discipline when new members join the church.* This teaching should deal with the scriptural basis for church discipline, God's purpose for it, and its limitations.

Guideline #7: *Always proceed in strict conformity with the rules of discipline adopted by the congregation.*

Guideline #8: *Keep the rolls of the church updated and accurate.* Always know who is a communicant member and therefore eligible to vote. Accurate rolls will make it possible to follow the details of parliamentary procedure and avoid many causes of tension, possible discipline and civil suits. This is especially true in determining quorums and the number of votes necessary for a motion to be passed. Each depends on the number of communicant members present, not on the number of people present.

Policies governing the removal of names from the roll should be stated in the bylaws. First, they should define who will be maintained as members in good and regular standing—normally those who attend church with some regularity when possible. (Note that a healthy church often has more people attending its services than are on the roll.) Second, the bylaws should state how often the roll will be reviewed. It is best to examine part of the roll each month, so that the entire roll is reviewed once a year. Third, the bylaws should state the reasons for removing names from the roll. Fourth, they should set forth the procedure for removing a name. The procedure should vary, depending on the reason for removal.

Guideline #9: *Prepare public statements about judicial matters very carefully*. Elders should not simply make spontaneous announcements. Rather, they should follow these instructions:

- Pray for wisdom and clarity beforehand.
- Write out the proposed announcement.
- Indicate in it how the members should govern their attitude toward, and relationship with, the offender while he is under censure.
- Support the announcement with comments on the biblical purpose for discipline.
- Evaluate the statement to determine if it communicates what is desired; if it does not, rewrite it.
- Use only the written text when making the announcement.
- Do not make additional "unofficial" comments.
- Normally, make announcements of this nature only to the members of the congregation.
- Do only what is announced in the statement.
- Keep the written statement in the minutes of the elders.

The elders must carefully consider how much detail to include in the announcement. As a rule of thumb, it is best to reveal as little detail as possible, while still being accurate and informative. For example, in his denunciation of a sin in 1 Corinthians 5:1, Paul states its precise nature and extent, but is careful to do so accurately. The elders should be prepared to follow up their statements with a shepherd-oriented ministry to church members.

Guideline #10: *Give strong and authoritative warning to the* church that the judicial announcement is only a statement of fact, a plea for prayer, and a guide for relating to the censured offender. This warning should add that any spreading of the details of the case to the general public, no matter how general the remarks may be, is gossip. As such, it subjects the gossipper to discipline.

Reference has been made to the Marian Guinn case. One of the major aspects of the case was the accusation by the offender that, in effect, she was slandered by the "gossip" of the elders to the congregation and to other congregations. By implication there was also the accusation that the church members spread it abroad.

Guideline #11: *Notify other churches in the denomination of any disciplinary action, if denominational law so requires.* This requirement is often restricted to action taken against ministers.

If notification is not required, the elders normally would only notify a church to which the person under discipline is seeking to escape. The elders must contact that church. They may choose to communicate only that the individual has not repented of proven sin and is under discipline, or they may go into all the details. They should warn the elders of that church that the individual cannot be received into its membership without dishonoring the name of Christ and marring the testimony of their church.

These guidelines may be concluded with this advice to the elders: Do your homework constantly and with great care in all matters of church life. Then, if judicial process is needed, proceed to censure the offender, depending on the grace of the Lord to care for his church just as you are depending on him to use the censure to bring the offender to repentance and restoration.

Questions for Reflection and Discussion

1. What are the practical implications of trying to keep the

vows that one has taken when joining the church? How can such vows be strengthened?

2. Why must church documents be used with great care? Illustrate this, using the bylaws of your church.

3. Why is it necessary to be very careful when issuing a public statement about a disciplinary matter? Think of a hypothetical case in which a church member has been censured, and prepare the first public announcement of the imposition of the censure.

4. How could the guidelines presented in this chapter have been used by the elders when they were confronted by the Marian Guinn case?

5. What lessons about church discipline may be learned from the Marian Guinn case?